D0860248

We're Heaven Bound!

DAY
HYMNS

We're Heaven Bound!

PORTRAIT OF A BLACK SACRED DRAMA

GREGORY D. COLEMAN

The University of Georgia Press
Athens and London

Published by the University of Georgia Press
Athens, Georgia 30602

Designed by Sandra Strother Hudson
Set in 10 on 14 Cheltenham Book by Tseng Information Systems, Inc.
Printed and bound by Thomson-Shore
The paper in this book meets the guidelines for permanence and durability of the Committee on Production Guidelines for Book Longevity of the Council on Library Resources.

Printed in the United States of America
98 97 96 95 94 C 5 4 3 2 1

Library of Congress Cataloging in Publication Data

Coleman, Gregory D.
We're heaven bound! : portrait of a Black sacred drama / Gregory D. Coleman.
p. cm.
Includes bibliographical references (p.) and index.
ISBN 0-8203-1684-9 (alk. paper)
1. Drama in public worship—History—20th century. 2. Christian drama—Presentation, etc. 3. Big Bethel African Methodist Episcopal Church—History—20th century. 4. Afro-American churches—Georgia—Atlanta—History—20th century. 5. Afro-American Methodists—Georgia—Atlanta—Religious life. 6. Atlanta (Ga.)—Church history—20th century. 7. Georgia—Church history—20th century.
I. Title. II. Title: We are heaven bound!
BV289.C65 1994
246′.7—dc20 94-15273

British Library Cataloging in Publication Data available

The Scroll Reading, reproduced in the introduction, is reprinted from Redding Suggs, "Heaven Bound," *Southern Folklore Quarterly* 27 (December 1963): 251–66, by permission.

Photographic restoration courtesy of Dr. W. Robert Nix, School of Art, University of Georgia.

Frontispiece: Henry Furlow as Satan. Furlow was the star of *Heaven Bound* for fifty years.

To
Shelia, Gerald, and Meredith—my wonderful wife, son, and daughter—whose love, patience, and encouragement are memorialized in these pages

The late William Coleman Sr. and Nannie Braswell Coleman—my parents—who fired my ambitions, gave me values, and brought me lovingly along the way

Sallie Daniel Braswell—my sainted grandmother—who explained to me the love of African Methodism in my blood for six generations

The old gang, now my fan club in the sky—Perry Jeff ("Pop") Daniel, Nathaniel ("Bud") Braswell, Kizzie ("Auntee") Daniel, Mattie Daniel Thurmond, Hattie Braswell Matthews, and Amanda Braswell Carnes

Big Bethel African Methodist Episcopal Church and the glory of African Methodism

Contents

Preface

The congregation of Big Bethel African Methodist Episcopal Church, a tremendous stone building on Auburn Avenue at the center of Atlanta, Georgia, has had its share of baptisms, weddings, conversions, and deaths. From the congregation's beginning in 1847, however, this far from ordinary flock has had a unique mission, and its dynamic pastors have been towers of leadership: prophets, bishops, educators, and civil libertarians. Bethel's members, luminaries in the Atlanta community, started schools and set up programs to bring about literacy and foster economic cooperation among newly freed slaves. Always skilled diplomats, Big Bethelites formed important alliances between the races and often hosted world leaders in their midst. Of all the triumphs in the history of this remarkable black church, however, one stands above all others. It is the internationally acclaimed morality play *Heaven Bound.*

Counting hundreds of thousands in its many audiences, the play exploits the powerful medium of black theater to depict the pilgrim soul on its way to Heaven. Despite the popularity of the play, the story surrounding its origin and development has remained, until now, untold. It was not that people did not want to know the story. Indeed, historians, musicians, folklorists, and others came calling many times to delve into the play's origins. The untrusting parishioners, however, were silent about the history of the play. Although strange and frustrating to outsiders, the silence existed for understandable reasons. Part of it was an effort by the congregation to forget a nasty fight about the *Heaven Bound* copyright that was waged in federal court in the early 1930s.

The choir member who brought the idea of the play to the church alleged that church officials used her play without her permission and without giving her royalties. The fight in the courts did not dispose of the copyright question, however, as nobody emerged with a registered copyright. The absence of a copyright in the church's name became an even stronger reason to continue the silence. Only by remaining silent was the church able to keep for itself the handsome revenues generated by the play, revenues vital in getting the debt-ridden church through the Great Depression. For many years, therefore, Big Bethelites said nothing to journalists, scholars, and others inquiring about the play's narration (called the scroll reading), the director's notes, the copyright, or even the song sheets. Not the slightest hint of a text or script would be given to other groups, broadcast evangelicals, or theater companies seeking to present the play.

While the extraordinary conspiracy of silence served its purposes in the early days, it later dimmed prospects for the play's survival. Theater and college drama groups, as well as foundations established to support the arts, gave up trying to persuade church officials to let the play be performed elsewhere. And scholars unable to learn details about the play left it out of anthologies and other compilations about black music and drama. The silence also caused a black-out of significant events of Big Bethel's history. For the story of *Heaven Bound* went far beyond the subtleties of copyright law or the advantages of keeping money flowing through the church. *Heaven Bound* was the soul of Big Bethel, the witness of its congregation in the world, the epitome of all that was good and daring in a band of common church people who started out as slaves. Many of the details of the story disappeared with the deaths of Big Bethelites who were around during the 1930s and 1940s. But much of the story can still be told by those of us who watched and listened and then remembered what the old-timers did and said.

Breaking the silence, therefore, I now attempt to tell the full *Heaven Bound* story, hoping to do justice to its truth and beauty. I also tell this story, hoping to honor that magnificent caravan of sainted pilgrims whose commitment and valor made the play great. To tell this story is a high and noble task, and I fervently thank Him who calls me to it.

Acknowledgments

For their thoughtful reading of the manuscript, which resulted in several adjustments of style and factual content, I am deeply indebted to my mother, Nannie Coleman, and my friend Pearlie Dove, both of whom are longtime members of the Big Bethel congregation and the *Heaven Bound* cast. I am also forever grateful to my wife, Shelia, who not only shared me generously for this venture but scrupulously read the manuscript and gave sound advice as to its ebb and flow. For her frank evaluation of the manuscript for the University of Georgia Press, I thank Winona Fletcher, professor of Theater and Afro-American Studies at Indiana University. I also thank Dennis Dickerson, historiographer of the African Methodist Episcopal Church and professor of history at Williams College, for his encouragement and for the indispensable guidance afforded in his research primer, *The Past Is in Your Hands.* Also deserving of mention is Sujette Fountain Crank, friend, trustee of Big Bethel Church, and a true daughter of African Methodism, who read the manuscript and summarized its content for Big Bethel's officers. Many thanks to my maternal aunts, Daisy Denson and Juanita Willis, on whose wise counsel I have relied in this and other worthwhile endeavors in my life. Last, but not least, I thank Mary Ruth Talmadge King, a longtime chronicler and archivist of Big Bethel's history, who shared lavishly from her vast storehouse of knowledge about the church's past and allowed me access to the scrapbook of Charity Collins Miles, her late aunt. The scrapbook included newspaper clippings chronicling *Heaven Bound* and the Big Bethel choirs during the 1930s and early 1940s and a clipping that places between 1940 and 1945 the injury of several Angels who fell from a poorly built platform at the Atlanta Municipal Auditorium.

We're Heaven Bound!

Introduction: The Scroll Reading

In 1931 *Theatre Guild* magazine called *Heaven Bound* "the first great American folk drama." A few months later, *Time* magazine echoed the enthusiasm, calling the new black folk play "part pageant, part revival meeting, part spiritual charades." In 1985, the *New York Times,* looking back on more than a half-century of performances put on for hundreds of huge appreciative audiences, hailed the play as "one of Atlanta's most enduring traditions."

Although *Heaven Bound* was written in 1930 by two members of Atlanta's oldest black congregation, the Big Bethel African Methodist Episcopal Church, the play actually arises out of the lives and souls of a race. Tapping into a universal fascination with the journey and fate of the pilgrim soul, this simple folk play tells a powerful story of the road to Heaven and the pitfalls along the way.

Far more than plot and set, the play unveils the consummate talent, personal hardships, and faithfulness of the entire caravan of people who are part of each annual production. Faithful but fumbling, proud but erring, each of these wonderful, imperfect human beings steps forward with his or her special piece of the cultural mosaic that might be called the *Heaven Bound* experience. The church members who are the play's Saints, Pilgrims, Angels, and other characters bring to their roles the unique dimension of their own predicaments. Using these predicaments to guide their dramatic instincts, these stunning actors transform the aisles of the church into a real stretch of Life's Highway.

Aside from its deeper meaning, *Heaven Bound* is good entertainment. The convincing drama and lilting spirituals flow naturally from the warmth and talent of the church's members, and the church's pulpit-in-the-round makes the sanctuary a handsome theater. The play's Pilgrims—twenty-four of them—come trudging around Big Bethel's huge white altar, depicting life's circumstances in all their variety. Nimble, cunning, and horned, Satan waylays all the Pilgrims but succeeds in spellbinding only a few. When a struggling Pilgrim overcomes satanic power and passes through the Pearly Gates, the Celestial Choir raises a mighty hymn of praise.

HEAVEN BOUND: THE SCROLL READING

The play is performed in pantomime and song, without the aid of a script. Following the lead provided by the hymns and spirituals sung, a narrator furnishes the continuity that weaves together the events of the play.

Scene

The auditorium of the Big Bethel African Methodist Episcopal Church, Atlanta. Clouds cut from white cardboard are attached to the pews of the Choir, facing audience, with Gates of Heaven set center. Hell is to the right of the audience, a curtained corner of the auditorium from which a red glow and occasional puffs of smoke issue.

1.

The Angels of the Celestial Choir are in Heaven, and the Narrator stands at lectern to the right. Angels with swords guard the Gates. All are gowned in white, with wings and golden crowns.

Persons of the Drama

The Narrator

St. Peter, St. Cecilia, Angels } The Celestial Choir
First Pilgrim
The Wayworn Traveller
The Pilgrim of the Cross
Satan
The Striver
The Wayward Girl
The Mother's Girl
The Rich Man
A Widow with Orphans
The Pilgrim of Faith
The Pilgrim to the Promised Land
Gamblers
Their Christian mother
The Pilgrim of Sorrow
A Determined Soul
The Preacher
The Hypocrite
The Bedridden Soul
The Burden-Bearer
A Reformed Drunkard
A Soldier in the Army of the Lord

Narrator: From eternity comes the sound of many voices, voices of the ransomed hosts of God, the saints and the angels. These are they which came out of the great tribulations and have washed their robes and made them white in the blood of the Lamb. They come singing—the songs of the sainted!

Enter rear right St. Peter with Keys and Book of Gold and bearded, followed by St. Cecilia with lyre leading a procession of Angels, all singing:

When the Saints go marching in,
O, when the Saints go marching in,
I want to be in that number
When the saints go marching in.

When they stand around the throne,
O, when they stand around the throne,
I want to be in that number
When they stand around the throne.

When they crown Him Lord of all,
O, when they crown Him Lord of all,
I want to be in that number
When they crown Him Lord of all.

2.

The procession having entered Heaven, St. Peter stations himself at the Gates.

Narrator: Heaven bound pilgrims of the earth hear a call—a distant cry from Heaven bidding them come.

Celestial Choir sings "When We All Get to Heaven."

Narrator: Above the noise and din of Earth—above the loud trafficking of souls echoes and re-echoes the rejoicing of the saints as they sing the love of Jesus, and shout their eternal victory.

Celestial Choir (singing):

Chariot rode on the mountain top,
God's going to build up Zion's walls!
My God spoke and the chariot did stop,
God's going to build up Zion's walls!

Chorus
Great Day! great day of the righteous marching,
Great Day! God's going to build up Zion's walls.

3.

Narrator: The ransomed of the Lord shall return and come to Zion with songs and everlasting joy upon their heads, they shall obtain joy and gladness, and sorrow and sighing shall flee away. One comes, a steadfast soul, beckoning to all who love the Lord, to follow in her footsteps and march to Zion.

Enter right rear, the First Pilgrim, a woman in a white robe and bearing a palm, beckoning as she sings "Come We That Love the Lord." The First Pilgrim enters Heaven.

4.

Narrator: And now is heard the cry of the footsore traveller, leaning heavily upon his stall, with ebbing strength. He braves the mountain, but is spurred on to the Golden Gates by a vision of palms of victory and a crown of glory.

Enter right rear, the Wayworn Traveller, an old man in tattered street clothes with staff; he walks painfully.

Celestial Choir sings "I Saw a Way-Worn Traveller." The Wayworn Traveller leads the Chorus. He enters Heaven where he receives robe and crown.

5.

Narrator: With eyes fixed steadfastly upon the cross, the sole object of her glory, comes a pilgrim to the gate of heaven. Because of her true and undying love for the cross of Jesus, she is admitted to the Holy City where crosses are exchanged for crowns.

Enter right rear, the Pilgrim of the Cross, a woman in white bearing with effort a cross.

Pilgrim of the Cross (singing):

I've a mother in the kingdom,
Ain't dat good news?
I've a mother in the kingdom,
Ain't dat good news?

Going to lay down this world,
Going to shoulder up my cross,
Going to take it home to Jesus,
Ain't dat good news?

Enter from Hell, Satan in red satin with horns, tail, and pitchfork, to sneak up ingratiatingly to the Pilgrim of the Cross only to cower as she repeatedly raises the cross above him and continues to sing:

I've a father in the kingdom,
Ain't dat good news?
I've a father in the kingdom,
Ain't dat good news?
Going to lay down this world, etc.

The Pilgrim of the Cross enters Heaven, where the Angels lift her cross and place a crown upon her head while Satan retires disgustedly into Hell.

6.

Narrator: Steadily tramping, forging his way toward the city of Zion, comes a staunch and true child of the King. The echo of his firm and steady tread rings out as he marches unscathed thru the fiery flames of Satan's temptations and succeeds in making Heaven his home.

Enter right rear, the Striver in white robe, plodding with exaggerated determination. Satan emerges from Hell, makes no serious attempt on the virtue of this obviously righteous man, but mimicks him disrespectfully.

The Striver (singing):

Haven't been to heaven but I've been told,
Trying to make heaven my home,
The streets up there are paved with gold,
Trying to make heaven my home.

Chorus
I'm tramping, tramping,
Trying to make heaven my home.

If you get there before I do,
(Trying to make heaven my home)

Tell all my friends I'm coming too
(Trying to make heaven my home).

Old Satan's just like a snake in the grass
(Trying to make heaven my home)
He's always in some Christian's path
(Trying to make heaven my home).

The Striver maintains his deliberate pace and enters Heaven.

7.

Narrator: What wayward frivolous soul cometh now to the gate of Heaven? She it is who has trod the primrose path, heeding not, caring not, as she quaffs the cup of pleasure to its dregs, she comes—begging admittance but alas! the gates are closed. She hears the echo of her own despairing cry—too late, too late!

Enter right rear, the Wayward Girl in evening gown. She is met confidently by Satan, who flirts with her. She responds boldly, raising from time to time a champagne glass while the Celestial Choir watch in horror. When she reaches the chancel rail, Satan turns ugly and begins urging her towards Hell with his pitchfork. She implores Heaven to save her but is run into Hell. The Celestial Choir hums.

Celestial Choir (bursting into full voice):

Don't let it be said, too late, too late
To enter the golden gate;
Don't let it be said, too late, too late
To enter the golden gate.

My mother she's gone, she's gone, she's gone
To enter the golden gate;
My mother she's gone, she's gone, she's gone
To enter the golden gate.

8.

Narrator: Like the light of a lone star on a dark night, mother love has shown in the life of this poor child. This love, beckoning and calling from beyond the grave, has led her to her Saviour, and now fully won by its tender plea, she cries—tell Mother I'll be there!

Enter right rear, the Mother's Girl, in white. The mother waits yearningly at the gate and watches in great concern as Satan repeatedly tempts the daughter with bright beads.

The Mother's Girl (singing):

When I was but a little child
How well I recollect,
How I would grieve my mother
With my folly and neglect;
And now that she has gone to heav'n
I miss her tender care:
O angels, tell my mother I'll be there.

Chorus
Tell mother I'll be there
In answer to her prayer
This message, guardian angels, to her bear
Tell Mother I'll be there
Heav'n's joy with her to share
Yes, tell my darling mother I'll be there.

One day a message came to me,
It bade me quickly come
If I would see my mother
Ere the Savior took her home:
I promised her, before she died,
For heaven to prepare:
O angels, tell my mother I'll be there.

To Satan's chagrin and the joy of the Angels, she resists the beads and is welcomed into Heaven by the mother.

9.

Narrator: To the golden gate with proud and haughty stride, with confidence in the power of his gold, comes the Rich Man. Rich—yes, in worldly goods, but poor, miserably poor, in love and compassion for his fellow beings. To the cries of the poor and defenseless, he has turned a deaf ear, but their cries shall not be in vain, for while their fate will be one of everlasting joy and gladness—his will be one of awful doom and eternal torment.

Enter right rear, the Rich Man in expensive double-breasted suit and ostentatious accessories, to encounter and ignore the Widow, in weeds, and her two Orphans, begging. Satan encourages his victim in this callousness.

Celestial Choir:

Come down, come down, my Lord, come down,
My Lord's writing all the time;
And take me up to wear the crown,
My Lord's writing all the time.

Chorus
Oh, He sees all you do and hears all you say,
My Lord's writing all the time.
When I was down in Egypt land,
My Lord's writing all the time;
I heard some talk of the promised land,
My Lord's writing all the time.

Satan drives the Rich Man into Hell

10.

Narrator: And lo! through the ages comes one who is full of faith—one who has laid his foundation on the word of God. The powers of sin and hell prevaileth not against him.

Enter right rear, the Pilgrim of Faith, a man in white robe whom Satan attempts to interest in worldly things by offering to deal him a hand of outsized cards.

The Pilgrim of Faith, accompanied by the Celestial Choir (singing):

Don't you let nobody turn you 'round, turn you 'round, turn you 'round,
Don't you let nobody turn you 'round,
Just keep on to Galilee.

Never weakening, the Pilgrim of Faith brushes Satan aside and enters Heaven.

11.

Narrator: To the gate of Heaven now comes a pilgrim who has overcome the powers of darkness through her hope and belief in a brighter future. She has cherished through long, bitter years this one desire to reach the land where temptations and sorrows never come.

Enter right rear, the Pilgrim to the Promised Land, a woman in white, whom Satan tempts with a fancy hat.

The Pilgrim to the Promised Land (singing):

Come and go to that land,
Come and go to that land,
Come and go to that land,
Where I'm bound, where I'm bound;
Come and go to that land,
Come and go to that land,
Come and go to that land where I'm bound.

No temptations in that land,
No temptations in that land,
No temptations in that land,
Where I'm bound, where I'm bound;
No temptations in that land,
No temptations in that land,
No temptations in that land where I'm bound.

I have a mother in that land (repeat)

I have a Savior in that land (repeat)

Peace and Joy in that land (repeat)

Repeatedly tempted, she repeatedly resists and disappoints Satan by entering Heaven.

12.

Narrator: Woe unto these gamblers, these evil doers, who care naught for their souls. One spurns the pleadings, the prayers, and the cries of their Christian mother, who attempts to turn him from the error of his ways. The other, of tender age, turns from his gaming and evil doing, rejoicing in the salvation of his soul, and walks the strait and narrow path to the beautiful heavenly gate.

Enter right rear, two Gamblers in flashy street clothes who play craps in the aisle with dice of exaggerated size while Satan eggs them on. Enter from front, the Christian mother, beseeching them to desist and courageously facing and insulting Satan.

The Christian Mother sings "I Am Praying for You" ("I Have a Savior").

The younger Gambler desists and marches off into Heaven while Satan drives the older into Hell and the emotions of the Christian Mother are divided.

13.

Narrator: A poor desolate soul reaches the gate of Paradise. Thru many troubles, trials and sorrows she has come. Nobody knew and nobody cared but Jesus.

Enter right rear, the Pilgrim of Sorrow, a woman in white robe with black kerchief on her head.

The Pilgrim of Sorrow (singing):

Oh! Nobody knows the trouble I've seen,
Nobody knows but Jesus;
Nobody knows the trouble I've seen,
Glory, hallelujah! (repeat)
Sometimes I'm up, sometimes I'm down,
Oh, yes, Lord!
Sometimes I'm almost to the ground,
Oh, yes, Lord!

The Pilgrim of Sorrow is too preoccupied to notice Satan, who indicates at first that he thinks her an easy mark; finally he lies on his back in the aisle with outspread legs resting on the arms of the pews. She steps over him as if he were not there.

14.

Narrator: And now comes one who is determined to go through with Jesus—with the Lord's despised few she has cast her lot, and is willing to pay the price, Old Satan without success tries to lure her from the path of righteousness.

Enter right rear, a Determined Soul, a woman in a white robe walking with decision. Satan, assessing her determination accurately, only half seriously accosts her.

A Determined Soul (singing):

> Lord, I have started to walk in the light,
> Shining upon me from heaven so bright,
> I've bade the world and its follies adieu,
> I've started in Jesus, and I'm going through.
>
> *Chorus*
> I'm going through, I'm going through,
> I'll pay the price, whatever others do;
> I'll take the way with the Lord's despised few,
> I've started in Jesus, and I'm going through.
>
> I'd rather walk with Jesus alone
> And have for my pillow like Jesus a stone;
> Living each moment with his face in view,
> Than turn from my pathway and fail to go through.
>
> O, brother, now will you take up the cross,
> Give up the world and count it but dross;
> Sell all you have and give to the poor,
> Then go through with Jesus and those who endure.

The Determined Soul moves undeviatingly into Heaven.

15.

Narrator: "Go ye into all the world and preach my gospel to every creature. Be ye steadfast, immovable, always abounding in the work of the Lord." This servant, faithful over a few things, presses on with the assurance of being made ruler over many.

Enter right rear, the Preacher, the actual minister of the church, in clerical garb, whom Satan tempts with money to no avail.

The Preacher and the Celestial Choir (singing):

> I'm going to do all I can for my Lord, for my Lord;
> I'm going to do all I can for my Lord, for my Lord;

I'm going to do all I can, till I can't do no more,
I'm going to do all I can for my Lord.

I'm going to pray all I can for my Lord (repeat)

I'm going to shout all I can for my Lord (repeat)

I'm going to preach all I can for my Lord (repeat)

I have done all I could for my Lord, for my Lord (repeat)

I have done all I could, and I can't do no more,
I have done all I could for my Lord.

Satan gives up in helpless disgust as the Preacher proceeds into Heaven.

16.

Narrator: How tragic is the fate of this creature—this vile pretender—this hypocrite. She of the pious face, prancing with the Devil and posing as a child of God at one and the same time. She proves an easy prey to all the blandishments of the evil one.

Enter right rear, the Hypocrite, an extraverted woman in red satin who flirts and takes a confident line with Satan while proceeding toward Heaven. Satan with knowing looks to the audience plays along until she reaches the gates, which the sworded angels bar. As the Hypocrite demands entry, Satan extends to her a wilted bouquet. She reaches for it and he drives her into Hell.

The Hypocrite (singing in ambiguous tones):

Sanctified and holy,
I shall not be moved,
Just like a tree planted by the water.

Chorus
Glory, Hallelujah, I shall not be moved,
Just like a tree planted by the water.

I want to go to Heaven,
Where I shall not be moved,
Just like a tree planted by the water.

If your mother forsakes you,
I shall not be moved, etc.
I am on my way to Heaven,
And I know I shall not be moved, etc.

17.

Narrator: Now comes a bedridden soul, who has suffered with patience her years of affliction. Nearing the end of life's weary journey, she wages a pitiful battle against the temptations of Satan. She implores the aid of the angels' band and they bear her away to her immortal home.

Enter right rear, the Bedridden Soul, a woman in an ordinary dress with cloth bandage on her head whom Satan sorely tempts with medicines. Half-way to Heaven, she manages to turn from Satan and raise her arms in supplication, whereupon the sworded Angels descend and carry her the rest of the way into Heaven.

The Bedridden Soul (singing):

My latest sun is sinking fast,
My race is nearly run;
My strongest trials now are past,
My triumph is begun.

Chorus
O come, angel band, come and around me stand,
O, bear me away on your snowy wings
To my immortal home.

I've almost gained my heav'nly home,
My spirit loudly sings;
The holy ones, behold, they come!
I hear the noise of wings.

18.

Narrator: To join the celestial host comes one bent beneath her burden of care. She stumbles and with slow sad steps wins her toilsome way to the Holy City—cheered on by the knowledge that one glorious day she will lay down her heavy load.

Enter right rear, the Burden Bearer in white robe with great heavy pack on her back, which Satan repeatedly offers to lift from her.

The Burden Bearer (singing):

Chorus

Oh, bye and bye, bye and bye, I'm going to lay down my heavy load.
Oh, bye and bye, bye and bye, I'm going to lay down my heavy load.

One of these mornings bright and fair
I'm going to lay down my heavy load;
Going to take my wings and cleave the air,
I'm going to lay down my heavy load.

Hell is a dark and deep despair,
I'm going to lay down my heavy load;
Stop, poor sinner, and don't go there,
I'm going to lay down my heavy load.

When I get to heaven going to sing and shout,
I'm going to lay down my heavy load;
There's nobody there to turn me out,
I'm going to lay down my heavy load.

The Burden Bearer insists on carrying the load to the gates, where she lays it down.

19.

Narrator: And now approaches one who was once a lover of strong drink—a slave to the bottle. Having turned from the error of his ways, he spends his time in prayer and meditation, trying to make it into the kingdom of Heaven. He wages a terrible battle with Satan, who tries to lure him into the gutter again to wallow in his debasement.

Enter right rear, the Reformed Drunkard in a white robe whom Satan almost persuades, again and again, to accept a bottle of whiskey, while the Celestial Choir watches in suspense. As the Reformed Drunkard begins to mount the short stairs which lead to the gates of Heaven, Satan all but forces him to take the whiskey. Meanwhile, the Celestial Choir becomes excited and begins to sing "Throw Out the Life Line," and one of the Angels throws a life preserver attached to a rope to the Drunkard who is then dragged into Heaven by the Angels as Satan hangs onto his coattails.

The Reformed Drunkard, safe in Heaven, joins the Choir.

The Reformed Drunkard with Celestial Choir (singing):

He saved me too, I'm of that number,
Bought by the Spirit and washed in His blood;
He saved me too, He saved me too,
Blessed be my savior,
For He saved me too.

20.

Narrator: A soldier of the army of the Lord comes, with a sword, warm from recent fight; though wounded and scarred, she finally obtains the victory.

Enter right rear, a Soldier in the Army of the Lord, with helmet, shield, and sword, and robed in white, who duels with Satan all the way to the gates of Heaven and there slays him.

The Soldier in the Army of the Lord (singing):

I'm a soldier in the army of the Lord,
I'm a soldier in the army;
I'm a soldier in the army of the Lord,
I'm a soldier in the army;

My mother lived and died in the army of the Lord,
My mother lived and died in the army;
My mother lived and died in the army of the Lord,
My mother lived and died in the army.

The Soldier enters Heaven and is crowned. Satan's body sprawls on the steps outside the gates.

Narrator: Soldier of God, well done! Rest from thy loved employ. The battle fought, the victory won, enter thy Master's joy.

21.

Narrator: And now, all the ransomed hosts of God are gathered with the angels. Their many voices are raised together in one glorious exultant hymn of praise. All glory, all honor, power to their Savoir, Lord, and King.

Enter from Hell, Satan, removing headgear and makeup, and the damned, to stand center front before the chancel rail.

Satan accompanied by the saved and the damned ensemble (singing):

All hail to Thee, Immanuel,
We cast our crowns before Thee;
Let every heart obey Thy will,
And every voice adore Thee.
In praise to Thee, our Savior King,
The vibrant chords of Heaven ring
And echo back the mighty strain:
All hail! All hail! All hail! All hail Immanuel!

Chorus with Soprano
Hail! Immanuel! Immanuel!
Hail!
Glory and honor and majesty,
Wisdom and power be unto Thee,
Now and evermore!
Hail! Immanuel! Immanuel!
Hail!
King of kings and Lord of lords,
All hail Immanuel!

Chorus with Alto and Bass
Hail to the King we love so well!
Hail! Immanuel.
Hail to the King we love so well!
Hail! Immanuel.
Glory and majesty,
Wisdom be unto Thee,
Now and evermore!
Hail to the King we love so well,
Hail! Immanuel.
Hail to the King we love so well,
Hail! Immanuel,
King of kings and Lord of lords,
All hail Immanuel.

Chorus with Tenor
Hail to the King we love so well, etc.

Chorus with Bass
Hail to the King we love so well, etc.

All hail to Thee, Immanuel,
The ransomed host surrounds Thee:
And earthly monarchs clamor forth,

Their sov'reign King to crown Thee.
While those redeemed in ages gone
Assembled round the great white throne
Break forth into immortal song.
All hail! All hail! All hail! All hail! All hail Immanuel.

All hail to Thee, Immanuel,
Our risen King and Savior;
Thy foes are vanquished, and Thou art
Omnipotent forever.
Death, sin, and hell no longer reign,
And Satan's power is burst in twain;
Eternal glory to Thy name:
All hail, etc.

22.

The Preacher (taking Narrator's place at lectern after removing costume): Ladies and gentlemen, the choir of the Big Bethel Church will close with a short concert of spirituals.

The ensemble sings a group of spirituals, usually "Steal Away to Jesus," "Swing Low, Sweet Chariot," "Study War No More," and with the performer who acted Satan as soloist, "Hand Me Down the Silver Trumpet, Gabriel."

Hope, Fun, Struggle, and Destiny: The *Heaven Bound* Experience

Like other literary and artistic works, *Heaven Bound* is a product of its history and environment. The prospect of Heaven as a force moving the entire pilgrimage of America's blacks from slavery into the twentieth century was the fundamental inspiration for the play. The past, therefore, is the prologue to the play, and Big Bethel Church, an agent of change and of African American uplift in the South, is its home.

The miraculous African American church in general, its faith, its strength, gives foundation to the play. Always at the hub of black existence, the pragmatic black church, especially in the segregated South of the early 1930s, offered a rare stage for blacks with artistic gifts and theatrical aspirations. It was in the church that black artists recited poetry, presented plays, and gave recitals. Unlike other budding biblical dramas that took on a commercial character and stayed on the theatrical circuit after World War I, *Heaven Bound* kept its home in the black church. Through its moving spirituals and hymns, the play reveals the poignant but unshakable black faith nurtured by the trials of slavery, the discrimination that followed, and the ever present need to "steal away to Jesus."

The play claims deep roots and rich heritage in the antebellum history of the congregation, as well as in the history of one of the great denominations of the black church—the African Methodist Episcopal Church, commonly known as the A.M.E. Church. Started in 1787, this black denomination grew out of a protest movement started by a group of former slaves led by Richard Allen, a man of remarkable courage and accomplishment. Allen taught himself to read and write and, after embracing the Christian faith, even converted his white master, who accepted Christ as his personal savior and model in life. After working long and hard to purchase his own freedom, Allen eventually organized the first national black convention, out of which he built the nationwide A.M.E. Church and became the first African American bishop.

Allen's bold movement to establish a separate black church at a time when slavery was an entrenched national institution was sparked by an incident in

Philadelphia's white Methodist Saint George's Church. During a worship service, a group of blacks ventured away from a gallery reserved for them and proceeded to the downstairs altar, where they knelt to pray. When asked by the whites to return to the gallery designated for them, the blacks refused. After finishing their prayers, the militants, led by Allen, filed out of the church and made plans to form a church of their own. For the next three-quarters of a century, the A.M.E. Church strengthened and grew, using as its organizational model the white Methodist church from which it had broken. The young denomination was organized into geographic districts headed by bishops elected by a central legislative body call the General Conference.

The early A.M.E. bishops were fearless visionary leaders obsessed not only with the spreading of the Christian gospel but with ideals of uplift that would bring literacy and culture to the race. These inspired bishops pushed the frontiers of their young church, first organizing congregations in the Northeast, then in the Midwest. Testing the waters in the days before the Civil War, the A.M.E. Church established congregations in the southern cities of Mobile, Savannah, and Charleston. But expansion in the South was cut short by southern slaveholders who viewed the educational programs of the church as a threat to the control of their slaves. Eventually, the Union army's victories in the Civil War opened to African Methodism the South and its vast population of former slaves. Between 1856 and 1876, the A.M.E. Church increased in size from twenty thousand to two hundred thousand members.

A national organization, the A.M.E. Church was uniquely situated to address a broader range of postslavery needs than were black Baptist churches or other single-unit organizations. The A.M.E.'s used the combined resources of their network of churches to look after the sick and the unemployed, and their printing press to encourage the rearing of black families and the establishment of black businesses. The young denomination also established schools almost everywhere it built a church, and published magazines and other literature on a nationwide basis. Wilberforce University, established in 1856 and taken over by the A.M.E. Church at the beginning of the Civil War, was one of the nation's first predominantly black colleges. And the *Christian Recorder,* an A.M.E. journal first published in 1847, was the first national black journal in the country. Before the end of the nineteenth century, the A.M.E.'s raised three seminaries, six high schools, and six colleges, mostly in southern states. One hundred years after the Civil War, the A.M.E. Church remained the largest corporate connection of blacks in America, embracing more than three million members and thousands of churches.

Although much of the early work of the A.M.E. Church centered on improving the earthly lot of African Americans, the chief concern of the church was to prepare its followers for an afterlife in Heaven. This obsessive outlook toward

Heaven could be traced back to the revolutionary thinking of the church's founder, Richard Allen. When elders in the white Methodist church threatened him with expulsion because of his determination to go ahead with a separate black church, he responded defiantly, "If you deny us your name, you cannot seal up the scripture and deny us a name in heaven." Allen's visions of Heaven inspired not only his thinking and his sermons but his music as well. According to the Harvard music historian Eileen Southern, Allen's compilation of hymns in the early 1800s was the first such volume used by northern black congregations in the new nation. In the hymnal, Allen specifically selected songs "to inspire his people to believe that their wretched existence on earth would be followed by a blissful one in heaven," said Southern.

Although the slaves in the South could not hear about Heaven from the A.M.E.'s or from any other source in the North until after the Civil War, they got their news in another way. A small number of southern slaveholders introduced their slaves to the Christian religion, sincerely believing that the souls of the slaves should be saved in Heaven. From the biblical lessons and hymns learned from the whites, the slaves fashioned their own music, centering much of it on themes of Heaven: "Heben, heben, evybody talkin 'bout heben ain't goin there, heben." "In dat great gittin up moanin, fare thee well, fare thee well." "Swing low sweet chariot, comin for to carry me home." In Heaven, there would be freedom, reunion with loved ones, and rest at last.

After Emancipation, the preoccupation with Heaven continued. Newly freed black preachers in the South frequently built their sermons around themes of the promised land. The promised land was not just an abstract Christian doctrine, but for many of those who experienced the earthly perils of being black, it was the only safe place to strive for. As the A.M.E. bishop and historian Richard R. Wright described it, black preachers told former slaves to "prepare for heaven by good conduct, godly relations one to another, by acting like their father, God . . . by soberness, less fighting etc." Thus, "getting to heaven," according to Wright, "became the greatest idea to enter the post Civil War Negro's soul."

Shortly after the Civil War ended, African Methodism spread across rural Georgia, reaching backwoods brush arbors and one-room churches warmed by potbellied stoves. The expanding church also went into the cities, where it found some black congregations already formed. Reaching Atlanta in 1865, an A.M.E. missionary, James Lynch, found two congregations made up of former slaves. One was Friendship Baptist Church, founded in 1862; the other was a black Methodist church called Bethel Tabernacle. Older than Friendship, the Bethel Tabernacle flock had formed in 1847, when a small group of slaves were allowed to worship in a white church called the Union Church, Atlanta's first church. When the slaves wanted to worship by themselves, they could do so in the evenings but only under the supervision of whites. Later, in 1855, the slaveholders permitted the slaves to build their own church, Bethel Tabernacle. Like the Union Church, Bethel Tabernacle was located in downtown Atlanta.

In 1866, a warm handclasp between Lynch and the Bethel Tabernacle pastor, Joseph Wood, brought the newly freed Bethel congregation into the A.M.E. denomination. Nowhere were the faith and spirit of African Methodism more alive than in the congregation that evolved from Bethel Tabernacle. Its history would be filled with glorious feats of uplift and progress for blacks. It would also be filled with challenges and setbacks that would test the will of the forward-looking congregation.

But these first Bethelites were fit for the stormy future before them. They had seen their helpless little Bethel church caught in the cross fire of the Civil War raging in Atlanta. The little church, once used as a smallpox hospital, barely escaped the fires of the Union army as it swept through the city in 1864. Three years after the war, Bethel Tabernacle's freedmen faced the challenge of building a larger church for their growing congregation. The new church, which would eventually be called Old Bethel, was built in 1868 on Old Wheat Street, now called Auburn Avenue.

In the late 1880s, the bulging Bethel congregation found itself building yet a fourth home—the mammoth Big Bethel. Undecided about going ahead with plans to build a new church, these Big Bethelites kept an all-night prayer vigil seeking divine guidance. Not long afterward, the gray stones of Big Bethel were being quarried at Georgia's nearby Stone Mountain and hauled in horse-drawn wagons to the site on Old Wheat Street. Gradually, the grand Victorian structure started to rise right next door to Old Bethel.

Although the goal was worthy, the building of Big Bethel seemed to start a new series of defeats. Upon its completion, the new sanctuary was plagued with structural problems. Twice it had to be rebuilt, once in 1891 and again in 1898. Both times, however, it was condemned as unsafe. Although continuing work made the huge church safe enough to be occupied in 1900, it was not completed—inside and out—until 1921. After more than thirty years and $300,000, Big Bethel was finally ready.

In 1923, a long nightmare of new troubles began. A monstrous fire broke out in the church office and spread throughout the building. The blaze left standing only the exterior walls and the facade of the new Moller pipe organ. The fire burned the roof and opened the church to the heavens. Adding misery to misery, the insurance on this new cathedral—one of the largest black-owned churches in the country—expired the day before the fire. To pay for rebuilding, it was necessary for the church to incur a tremendous debt.

It was during the congregation's struggle to reduce this debt that the idea of *Heaven Bound* was hatched. The play was to be a fund-raiser to help pay for the newly rebuilt Big Bethel. Quickly, the idea became reality, and performances drew huge audiences and raised a good bit of money. The rapid success of the play fulfilled the hopes of its authors beyond their wildest expectations. Into the history of Bethel Church, into its trials and tribulations, the play folded and blended itself. For thousands of people *Heaven Bound* became synonymous with Big Bethel. The church's needs were the play's reason for being, the parishioners were the play's stars, and the quaint chancel, its Heaven. *Heaven Bound* also reflected the strength, faith, and genius of the fallen slaves, as well as the pride and independence of African Methodism. Written at the dawn of the Great Depression, the play also revealed the heavenward outlook still guiding the pilgrimage of America's blacks, who had come from eighteenth-century slavery and emancipation into the period after World War II.

The long nightmare of slavery, the thirst for learning, the new responsibilities of freedom and citizenship, the establishment of schools, the building of churches, and the reconstitution of black families inspired the creation of *Heaven Bound.* Yes, there had to be a Heaven—to sing about, to preach about, to shout about, and, with the new black literacy of the 1920s, to write about.

The Making of a Play

It was along about the first of . . . November or October . . . 1929. . . . It was down stairs in the lecture room at choir rehearsal . . . all the choir members were there. . . . They didn't seem to want to take the play thinking it wouldn't be much, that there wasn't anything to it hardly. . . . I told them I had a play that I wanted the choir to put on . . . and told about all the characters, the Celestial Choir and all the characters coming in . . . and told her [the chorister] . . . some of the songs for them to sing as they came in. . . . I told them I thought that it [the play] would help to make money for the church and put them out of debt, they owed so much.—Lula Byrd Jones

Heaven Bound is a sacred play. . . . It portrays the struggles and pitfalls which beset poor sinful mortals striving to enter the golden gates of the promised land.—Nellie L. Davis

BIG BETHEL AND ITS MEMBERS—THE TWENTIES

By 1929 Big Bethel had recovered from the fire that nearly destroyed it six years earlier. What once had been a grandiose Victorian structure was now a two-thousand-seat Romanesque Revival marvel. For its stalwart members, the church was a source of pride and a symbol of adversity overcome. The restored blue neon letters carrying the message "Jesus Saves" were once again emblazoned on the spire. Auburn Avenue was a vibrant, thriving center of social and commercial activity and a place where all aspects of black culture met. Big Bethel was a church of the neighborhood, a church within walking distance of most of its members. The finest of the stately black sanctuaries on Auburn Avenue, Bethel gave grace and dignity to the thoroughfare. Like all strong black churches, Bethel Church was the hub of the black community. It was a church of leaders and a place where much of the civic business of the race was transacted. In the large sanctuary, town meetings often addressed matters of health, voting, economic security, and education for all the blacks in the city.

Above: The oldest congregants, circa 1920. *Below:* The men of Big Bethel, 1930.

The church in the 1920s was not oblivious to the world beyond its doors. The nation was between wars and was the new military leader in the Western world. Patriotism and national pride soared. And the population's spirit was bolstered by a booming economy. The automobile, just headed for mass production, was a rarity among the congregants. Radios were scarce, and motion pictures, especially the ones with sound, were a novelty. Ice refrigeration and kerosene lighting were still regarded as modern conveniences by some members of the church.

By 1929 the church's membership consisted of a wide range of people, young and old, well off and poor, educated and illiterate. A small portion of the congregation was quite well educated, and these members spread their learning to others in the church. They walked and talked distinctively and emulated such well-known black educators as W. E. B. Du Bois and Booker T. Washington. So rare was the opportunity for advanced formal training that academic degrees earned by black college graduates were affixed to their names in church bulletins and other publications circulating among blacks: "H. J. Furlow, A.B." and "W. A. Fountain, M.A." was how the church bulletin referred to two of its lettered members and clerics. Such conventions among blacks were, in those days, not so much a form of snobbery as an announcement that these people were "up from slavery."

Because Emancipation had occurred only a generation before, it was still common in the 1920s to find former slaves in the congregation. Some of the slaves had worshipped in Old Bethel, the church built in 1868. And several had even come from Bethel Tabernacle, the pre–Civil War church of Big Bethel's original congregation. Many of these old members felt that former enslavement was a badge of shame and was not to be talked about, so they just remembered it. But other slaves passed along the history and heritage of the race in their stories and their songs. Lydia Butler, a former slave affectionately called Mother Butler around the church, would gather the church's children around her and tell them stories of her childhood enslavement—stories they would never forget.

The presence of these former slaves would not let the flock forget the long treacherous road the slaves had traveled and the almighty God who had brought them along the way. Among the former slaves in the congregation were Mother Lou McNeal, the cook for former governor John Slaton, and J. S. Simonton, Knight Darden, David T. Howard, and Cornelius King, all church officers. Although officially emancipated, many of the former slaves remained in a form of servitude, working as domestic servants for whites. Only a few could claim any measure of wealth and prosperity. Whatever their social progress, though, all the former slaves must have been happy to be free, for anything was better than a life of bondage.

With a full cross-section of blacks from the local community, Bethel Church seemed to be "filled with the spirit." For Sunday morning worship, the church was packed, on the main floor as well as in the balcony. Pastor B. G. Dawson, noted for fine sermons, preached above the ringing bells of streetcars pulling into the streetcar barn just across the street from the church, behind Yates and Milton's drugstore. Despite the noise outside, the congregation was not distracted, and the church's worship services were fiery and jubilant. The members struggled all week long to make ends meet but on Sunday mornings would shout and rise to sing their favorite hymns. Mother Green Holmes, unabashed in her religion, would get happy and line out her favorite song, "When the Mists Are Rolled Away." And Mother Butler, her voice roaring like a lion, would burst into Big Bethel's aisles singing "Prayer Is the Key That Opens Heaven's Door."

SINGING FOR MONEY

The restoration of the fire-ravaged church drew blood, sweat, and tears from the members. J. A. Lankford, a black architect, estimated the damage at $135,000. Although part of the money to rebuild the church came from small donations and larger philanthropic gifts, much of the funds had to be borrowed. A $65,000 mortgage was taken out with the Citizens and Southern Bank of Atlanta, and all the church's debts were consolidated. Exhaustion from the rebuilding campaign brought R. H. Singleton, the church's young pastor in the early 1920s, to his death. "Money, money, and more money" was the church's constant plea.

To pay off the debt, several fund-raising attempts were made before the *Heaven Bound* idea surfaced. One, the suggestion of a white banker who extended loans to the church, was the formation of the Big Bethel Concert Choir. This new group was a combination of Big Bethel's two major choirs: Choir Number One and Choir Number Two, which were formed in 1918 with the division of the original Big Bethel Choir. Number One, as it came to be called, included several senior members from the original choir, while Number Two was a collection of some of the younger adult talent in the church. The combined choir—the Big Bethel Concert Choir—proved an important precursor of *Heaven Bound.* The choir specialized in singing spirituals, which it gleefully pumped out for gatherings around the city. The group not only raised a good bit of money but spread the church's reputation for fine choral music all over town. The money raised by the Concert Choir, however, was not enough to disperse the overhanging cloud of debt. Nor was relief to come from the meager resources of the members or from the numerous fund-raising rallies put on by the church's auxiliaries. Divine intervention was needed. It was in this atmosphere of urgency and need that prayers went up and the *Heaven Bound* idea emerged in a choir rehearsal in 1929.

MISS LULA BYRD AND HER IDEA

Lula Byrd Jones, affectionately called Miss Lula Byrd around the church, was born in Fort Gaines, Georgia, during the 1870s. In 1892, she moved to Atlanta and soon afterward joined Big Bethel. In 1900 she joined the newly organized Big Bethel Choir to sing alto.

In 1916 Jones fell in love with and married a fellow choir member, a tenor by the name of Henry Jones. A young schoolteacher, Henry was the widowed father of two young children, Thelma and Henry Jr. An effective disciplinarian and an excellent cook, Lula Jones was a good mother figure for the children and a fitting companion to her new husband.

After a seven-year stay in Tennille, Georgia, a small country town where Henry taught in a one-room school, the Joneses returned to Atlanta in 1925. Lula then went to work as a spotter at the Excelsior Laundry, and Henry landed a job as a substitute teacher. The Jones family immediately resumed membership in Bethel Church, where Lula and Henry joined Choir Number One, an offshoot of their old Big Bethel Choir. Henry Jr. joined the Junior Choir.

Seeing the financial devastation left in the wake of the fire, Lula Jones began thinking of ways to raise money. She tossed around several ideas with Belle Thomas, a coworker at the laundry. *Queen Ester, The Womanless Wedding,* and *The Lilliputian Wedding* were mock dramas that they discussed, but Jones finally settled on the idea of a procession of Heaven-bound pilgrims struggling mightily against Satan to make Heaven their home.

Even before Jones could piece her idea together and get it to the church, she met a skeptic in her niece, Mary Brinkley. Brinkley lived in the apartment above Jones's, not far from the church. Brinkley went downstairs to Jones's bedroom one night to ask Jones what she was writing. When Jones responded that it was a play to be used at the church, Brinkley reacted with some doubt. "To tell you the truth, I laughed at it . . . because I did not think it was any good," Brinkley later recalled.

But Jones was not discouraged. One night in November 1929 she went to a choir rehearsal with the *Heaven Bound* idea on her mind. H. M. McBride, an insurance collector for Atlanta Life and the chorister of the Big Bethel Choir in 1915, recalled the occasion: "Well, she outlined it. She said she would select

Lula Byrd Jones, circa 1915.

different characters, one to be known as the devil, who would be dressed in a peculiar costume . . . and other characters . . . angels . . . the celestial choir . . . a character known as St. Peter. . . ."

Although the entire choir had heard about Jones's proposal for a play, there was no real movement until the chorister, Nellie Lindley Davis, took up the idea. Davis, a young woman in her twenties, was an English teacher who also enjoyed singing and playing the piano. Because married African American women could not teach children attending Atlanta's daytime public schools, Davis taught adults attending night school. To Jones's idea, Davis put her own formal training, her authority as the choir leader, and her talent for writing eloquent prose. It was the combined talents of Davis and Jones, two stalwarts of Big Bethel's Choir Number One, that gave birth to the great *Heaven Bound.*

THE PLAY TAKES FORM

The developing play closely followed the idea Jones originally presented to the choir. There would be gates to Heaven, four Angels, and a Celestial Choir singing while marching to a promised land located in the choir loft. After the choir was seated in Heaven, ten Pilgrims appearing in sequence would portray diverse circumstances in life—alcoholism, upward struggle, solitude, orphan-

"Heaven Bound"

This is a sacred play introduced by Mrs Lula Byrd Jones
and the readings between the
pilgrims by Mrs Nellie L Davis and
Copyrightted by Choir NO. 1. of Big
Bethel A.M.E church, Atlanta, Ga

To perform this play there
should be thirty or thirty-five in
the group of men and women.

This group is divided into a
Celestial Chorus, pilgrims, angels,
St Peter and the Devil.

The Celestial chorus comes from
behind screen or from without
dressed in white Robes and golden
crowns with stars and on their
way to Heaven led by St peter and
six Angels all singing "When The Saints
Go marching In"

A distinct and clear reader
fore tells the coming of this procession

There is a Golden gate which marks the
entrance to Heaven, St peter is on the
inside of Gate with Record of Names

Original *Heaven Bound* notes for Choir Number One.

hood, tenacity, hypocrisy, and so forth. Each Pilgrim would sing a verse as part of his or her act, and the choir would join in the chorus. The only plot would be the conflict between the devil and the Heaven-bound Pilgrims.

The first performance was informal. Most of the Pilgrims had no specific titles but were simply called Pilgrims to Heaven. The original Drunkard, Wayward Girl, and Satan, however, were characters conceived by Jones and were in the play from the first performance. The church members who made up the cast originated parts of the play themselves. With leeway from chorister Davis to select various characters they wanted to see included in the drama, the players experimented with potential Pilgrims and came up with some good ideas. The all-time favorite, Hypocrite, for example, was an idea of the players.

The dramatic interpretations of all the characters were largely ad-libbed. Although this free-wheeling, do-your-own-thing style would be kept within bounds after the first performances, it turned out to be the genius of the play. It was this informality that allowed the play to take on the character and colorful raw talent of the common people who made up most of the cast.

Although Jones was the person who presented the *Heaven Bound* notion to the choir, it was Davis who was firmly in charge and who clarified Jones's ideas to the choir members. Davis liked Jones's suggestion of gates for Heaven, but she rejected Jones's idea of covering the gates with flowers. Drawing on her training as an English teacher and her knowledge of literary art form and drama, Davis also wrote the Scroll Reading, the narrative that was to be used as the continuity between the acts and songs of the various Pilgrims. Davis also put more action in Jones's play by adding a character called the Victor, later known as the Soldier in the Army of the Lord, who engaged the devil in full battle.

Saint Peter, a role played by Henry Matthews, a former slave, was an integral part of the first production, although it was not clear who wrote him in the play. In what may have been a prelude to the lawsuits that were to flare up over the copyright to the play, both Davis and Jones claimed to have originated the idea of a Saint Peter. But disagreement, if there was any, was hushed during the preparations for the first performance.

As the choir members prepared for their new roles, some showed innate talent. Ruby Lloyd, the choir secretary, was an Angel, one of the original four "seraphim and cherubim." She suited her role just fine, with her own long silky white hair and her crepe paper wings. In later years, Lloyd played Saint Cecelia and then was the Scroll Reader, or narrator.

The first Scroll Reader, Estella Wright, was a young college-bound soprano drafted from the Junior Choir. With clear diction and a resonant voice that filled the large auditorium, Estella brought the words of the Scroll alive for an attentive audience. She and her twin sister, Esther, were two of the youngest players in the drama and before appearing in the play had already sung duets in Sunday morning worship services. Esther, who after marrying became Esther McDonald, would one day have the enviable distinction of being the last surviving member of the original cast.

Except for the twins, all the Pilgrims and first singers in the Celestial Choir came from Bethel's Choir Number One. It was a hardy group with gifted voices, a talent for mimicry, and esprit de corp. As a Pilgrim to Heaven, Esther Jordan, a laundry worker who joined Number One, sang "I'm Going Through" in her thunderous contralto. The part of the Victor was played by Sarah Williams, a tall, red-headed soprano. Williams, when just a girl, had been recruited to sing at the church by Mother Lettie Crawford, who had heard her singing in the neighborhood where they both lived. Mamie Cleveland, another Number One faithful, was busy rehearsing for the role of an Angel in Heaven. It was Cleveland who would throw out the first lifeline to the desperate Drunkard. Her act of reeling the Drunkard into the promised land was tense and thrilling, as old Satan almost catches his prey. H. M. McBride was asked to play Satan, but he refused. Instead, George Pullum, a railroad clerk, took the part.

Hannah Lovelace, the original Deceiver, considered various costumes that might help her portray her character in the play. A white dress, she thought, would bring out the innocence and purity that she portrayed. John Bigsby, who married Pastor Singleton's widow, played the Wayworn Traveller, while Nellie Davis played the frivolous Wayward Girl. The rest of the Pilgrims—Belle Hubbard, Christine Lloyd, and others—put their best feet forward portraying characters not yet fully developed for this first performance.

All the songs used in the play were part of the then-current repertoire of the choirs. Although both Jones and Davis suggested songs for each Pilgrim's journey, they left it largely to the Pilgrims to select their own songs, just as those Pilgrims had selected some of the characters. Before the play grew to include more spirituals, most of the songs chosen for the first productions were old Methodist hymns. Such hymns as "The Unclouded Day," "The Old Rugged Cross," "How Firm a Foundation," and "I Dreamed the Great Judgement Morning," though part of the first performance, did not survive the play's first decade. Other favorites, however, like "Come We That Love the Lord," "Don't Let It Be Said Too Late, Too Late," "Throw Out the Lifeline," and "When the Saints Go Marching In," stayed with the play and are still sung today.

Fannie Nix, although not a member of the church, took her place in Big Bethel's extended church family as a devout member of the Daughters of Bethel, a beneficial society organized during Reconstruction to care for sick and aging former slaves. As the time drew near for the first performance, it was Nix who came up with a good idea for a costume for Satan. When one of the players went to Nix's house to talk about an appropriate costume for the play's principal character, Nix showed her visitor a small plastic statue of the devil. Bought in a dime store, it had a tail but no horns and was the model for the costuming of the first devil.

Although the play was almost ready after two months and five rehearsals, it still had no name. Lula Jones suggested "The Heaven-Bound People," but Nellie Davis, ever editing the ideas of others, abbreviated Jones's title for the play. It was to be *Heaven Bound.* "In thinking of the pilgrims . . . the ones that was going to heaven . . . I thought that name would suit nicely," Jones recalled.

THE FIRST PERFORMANCE

Like the message itself, everything about the presentation of the play was uncomplicated. Davis's early notes described a simple set and setting that called for few embellishments to the celestial motif that was already part of the church's architecture: "Time: Eternity . . . Scenery . . . A golden gate with arch overhead . . . Palm trees scattered about . . . Off to the side may be stretched a screen . . . behind which Satan will thrust his victims."

A Sunday morning church bulletin announced the first performance of the play, February 17, 1930. Money was scarce, so there were no printed programs, no drama consultants, no media experts, no lavish curtains to raise. The immense popularity that was soon to come was still a wish, and a quiet optimism filled the air.

As night fell that cold Monday, members of the Celestial Choir made ready, donning their gold crowns, white wings, and white robes laced with purple. Clara Edwards, a music teacher who had served the church for a long time as its organist, took her familiar seat at the grand Moller pipe organ. And then, with these exhilarating lines, the play began: "From eternity comes the sound of many voices, voices of the ransomed hosts of God, the saints, the angels."

Clutching a huge golden book containing the names of the Pilgrims to be admitted to the promised land, Saint Peter, convincingly played by Brother Matthews, was the first to arrive in Heaven to open the Pearly Gates. A much admired and respected member of the church, Matthews, Big Bethel's caretaker, had been the bell ringer in Old Bethel. Already a very old man with a long white beard, Matthews was perfect for the role of Saint Peter.

After Saint Peter's arrival in Heaven came the Angels and then the Celestial Choir, whose members carried palms as they marched through the aisles of the church singing the spiritual "When the Saints Go Marching In." After the choir was seated in Heaven, the spotlight turned to Lula Jones, who was, appropriately, the first Pilgrim to appear. With arms outstretched toward the promised land, she struck out down Life's Highway singing "Come We That

Love the Lord." Her leading role would later become known as the Pilgrim to Zion. After Jones, Satan, played by George Pullum, made his entrance. Pullum, by all accounts, made a convincing Satan, taunting and waylaying all the Pilgrims.

The first performance of *Heaven Bound* was presented with a cast of only thirty-four. The admission fee was ten cents per person, and the house was packed with more than two thousand new fans. At the time, no one could see the great fame that waited around the corner, but because of this new play, Big Bethel Church rose in its status among churches.

A Firm Foundation, A Great First Year

The emphasis blacks placed on education during the sixty years following the Civil War brought them to new levels of articulateness after the turn of the century. Following the end of World War I, an explosion of literary and artistic expression came out of the black experience and found its way to the printing presses of large urban centers. Poetry, songs, plays, and novels poured out from a new class of educated black writers. Even in the performing arts, music, and light entertainment, blacks during this period expressed themselves in a unique way. Much of this expression reflected the bitterness of slavery and the racial and economic oppression that followed. A good bit of it also reflected the firm black faith in a heavenly reward to come. Because the fully developed black society in Harlem was the center of this literary and artistic activity, the period is commonly referred to as the Harlem Renaissance.

A good amount of the intellectual traffic generated by the Harlem Renaissance came to Atlanta. Several of the movement's leading writers had connections in the city. James Weldon Johnson, one of the greatest writers of this period, graduated from Atlanta University. W. E. B. Du Bois, a prolific writer and one of the intellectual fathers of the movement, taught at Atlanta University, and Langston Hughes, the renowned Harlem poet, lectured there. Moreover, black scholars in the local black colleges were bringing back something special from the integrated universities in the North, where they went for advanced academic training. They were bringing back a new respect for the power of the pen and a new enthusiasm for black literature.

Making its debut in 1930, *Heaven Bound* joined several other works of the Harlem Renaissance that portrayed blacks' conceptions of the road to Heaven. James Weldon Johnson's sermonic poetry collection *God's Trombones* and his *Saint Peter Relates an Incident of Resurrection Day* were among those works. Appearing in 1932 were Countee Cullen's poem "Black Christ" and his novel *One Way to Heaven.* Other works, such as the plays *All God's Chillen Got Wings,* by Eugene O'Neill, and *In Abraham's Bosom,* a Pulitzer Prize winner by Paul Green, were written by white dramatists who were drawn to black culture.

Several of these works, performed at major New York theaters, boosted the careers of black actors.

Nellie Davis was no doubt in touch with the powerful new black literacy and the literature it produced. She was an intellectual who traveled to the North for advanced academic studies in her field. It was less certain that Lula Jones, an unlettered woman, consciously viewed her work as joining a larger school of dramatic works. What was certain was that the same painful past and daily struggles, the same faith, the same visions of Heaven that motivated other authors of this period motivated and influenced Jones as well.

The work with which *Heaven Bound* was most often compared was *The Green Pastures,* written by Marc Connelly, a white man. *The Green Pastures* was first presented on February 26, 1930, nine days after *Heaven Bound* was first performed. Both works centered on themes of Heaven and both featured spirituals and exploited black folkways as a dramatic style. After reviewing *The Green Pastures* a few months earlier, *Time* magazine, in 1931, called *Heaven Bound* "a genuine all-Negro product of the same kind [as *The Green Pastures*]." A year after the two plays debuted, the *Atlanta Daily World* reported, "*Heaven Bound* is rivaling *Green Pastures* for national favor." Although the similarities of the two plays were often cited, there were significant differences. *The Green Pastures* based its action on Old Testament biblical scenes and conformed its characters to racial stereotypes. *Heaven Bound,* on the other hand, depicted the lives of everyday people struggling to make Heaven their home. There were no celestial fish fries or spoken dialect in Big Bethel's play.

The Green Pastures, moreover, was more cosmopolitan than *Heaven Bound.* Taking off like wildfire in the North and West, Connelly's play gained an international reputation after playing on New York's Broadway and in theaters of several of the nation's large cities. Even a movie would be fashioned after this well-known play. But *Heaven Bound* competed as best it could in the provincial South, and in its early years, it created quite a stir.

THE RAVE OF ATLANTA

Perhaps it was the isolation of home life that helped make *Heaven Bound*'s first year an overwhelming success in Atlanta, as the play encouraged people to leave home for an evening of fun and spiritual uplift. Everybody, it seemed, was curious about Big Bethel's new Heaven, which was taking in Pilgrims before overflowing audiences, down on Atlanta's Auburn Avenue.

Heaven Bound's simplicity gave it an easy, wide appeal. The audience was so impressed with the first performance that eight additional performances followed within the next year. Choir Number Two was called upon to join Choir

Page 10 The Atlanta Journal

Big Bethel *Gives* Opera

"Heaven Bound" Has Attracted Such Attention That Nine Performances Have Been Given Here to Capacity Audiences. The Choirs at Big Bethel Are Now Contemplating a Series of Concerts to Be Held Every Third Sunday in the Month

RGARET HAMILTON RICHARDS

)PERA, as sung by the combined choirs of the Big Bethel African Methodist Episcopal Church, is becoming popular Atlanta.

he ninth presentation of "Heaven nd," staged by these singers last Friday st, is eloquent testimony to the fact that, le Atlanta likes its Metropolitan grand ra in the spring, it is quite capable of reciating an innovation in musical offer-, particularly when such a novelty has origin here at home.

ig Bethel choirs have sung spirituals and ins for many years with unqualified suc-, but "Heaven Bound" is their first effort ard combining dramatics and creating an era.". When it had been presented six s and the public still clamored for e, the Auditorium-Armory was engaged its seventh performance, October 10, on [illegible] the house was packed from stage to rafters, and hundreds, some thousands, were turned away. The e section of seats reserved for white per- was likewise filled to overflowing. ent encores brought another presenta- on October 23, when an estimated d of 4,000 attended. It was at the re- t of the St. Mark's Methodist Church, Peachtree Street, that the ninth per- ance was staged Friday night at Big hel.

And now," declared the Rev. B. G. Daw- pastor of Big Bethel, "'Heaven Bound' oing into winter quarters."

ther questioning developed the fact he pastor and the choir are consider- itional plans for furnishing Atlanta ical treats of unusual flavor. They plan the Big Bethel Choir on a choral organizations in other cities, ging at certain hours during the onsored by large choirs for the music lovers. While these plans en completed, the Big Bethel mplate giving a concert one [illegible] in each month. [illegible] [illegible] flict with the [illegible] of any n or organization in the city. ld be mailed during the week Bethel office, for the choir likes and it enjoys nothing more than the wishes of its white patrons.

n Bound" is, as intimated, a local n, written and directed by Nellie graduate of Atlanta University and er in the David T. Howard School. directors of the Big Bethel choir are Massey and Josephine Bigboe, both duats" of Spelman College. "Heaven nd" portrays the struggles and pitfalls h beset poor, sinful mortals striving to r the golden gates of the promised land. ne member of the choir advertised it to employers, "There's some hellbound in n," for the devil, red, sly and cunning, ways tempting the weak pilgrims to from the straight and narrow path. e fight him valiantly and thrust him to receive their triumphant crown at golden gates, but, with some, his en- e seductive grins and bribes succeed, pathetic groans echo through the galleries as he gleefully pushes them through the portals of hell.

Big Bethel Church.

The Devil, although he does not sing a note, was one of the hits of the play, and brought down the house by his "devilish" actions, his broad smile and his clever pantomime. George Pullum, who plays this character, is a mail clerk. The Rev. Dawson explained that he has a splendid voice and is one of the best basses in the choir and that he also sings a good "soprano." All of the singers are hard-working men and women; some of them are college graduates, but the majority are porters, postal employes or domestic helpers. They sing because they love it, and as one of them said, they could put on "Heaven Bound" at a moment's notice without rehearsal. The Rev. Dawson announced that any time visitors from another section of the United States desired to hear real southern "darkies" sing, they would gladly accommodate them.

Although too busy with his ministerial duties to join the choir, the Rev. Dawson also is a musician. Big Bethel is rightfully proud of the beautiful pipe organ in the church, and the pastor demonstrated its splendid tone qualities by playing several selections for the benefit of the interviewer, who enjoyed them immensely. The church has a seating capacity of 2,000, with special pews reserved each Sunday for white friends. Dawson is a graduate of Morris Brown and attended Tuskegee, Columbia University and several other well-known colleges. He was formerly pastor of a large church in Chicago.

The Atlanta World, a negro newspaper, reported "Heaven Bound" as follows: "One should not marvel over the fact that this play continues to pack the house to capacity at each performance, for the religious fervor resultant from such inspired singing gives a certain spiritual rejuvenation that stirs the emotions of the coldest soul and reaches out with a cry for more. The characterization of the pilgrims journeying to the golden gates showed masterly directing; their singing along the highway to heaven brought moments of pathos, and with some, moments of humor, as the devil continues his variety of temptations."

[illegible] first [illegible] performance the "religious fervor" was [illegible] potent, for one dusky damsel in the orchestra section "got happy" and shouted lustily. The choir sang on, in an effort to appear nonchalant, and four stalwart "brothers" struggled vainly to hold her quiet, but shout she would until the "happiness" passed, leaving her limp and trembling. "It's jus like regular campmeetin'," one beaming sister remarked.

Negro singing is difficult to describe. It is like no other harmony. The haunting sweetness, the sustained notes, the swinging, lilting rhythm and the repetition of phrases with the varied shadings and control of tone produce a musical picture of rare charm and poignant beauty. Atlanta audiences, true to operatic form, refused to leave at the conclusion of the numbers and insisted upon old favorites, which were graciously accorded. "Swing Low, Sweet Chariot," was sung as few audiences have been privileged to hear it. It is a safe bet that if the winter concerts honor all requests, "Swing Low" will appear on every program.

"Big Bethel *Gives* Opera," *Atlanta Journal,* November 1930.

Number One, thus enlarging the play's Celestial Choir as well as providing a pool of alternate singers to meet the hectic demand. The *Atlanta Journal* gave an account of the play's first year: "Big Bethel's choirs have sung spirituals and hymns for many years with unqualified success, but *Heaven Bound* is their first effort toward combining dramatics and creating an 'opera.' "

Henry Jones Sr., the husband of Lula Jones, recalled the time during the play's first year when *Heaven Bound* had already outgrown the two-thousand-seat sanctuary of Big Bethel Church: "Seemingly we did not know where to put it on in a bigger way and it was being asked for by several churches. . . . The plan I devised was to have fifteen churches sponsor a performance . . . at the [Atlanta Municipal] auditorium. The cast and choir in the play was augmented and the number of people on the stage was necessarily about 200." Eight thousand people, reported *Time* magazine, saw this seventh performance of the play in October 1930. An additional five thousand, according to *Time,* were turned away at the door. The *Atlanta Journal* reported that "the house was packed from backstage to rafters and . . . urgent encores brought another presentation . . . when an estimated crowd of 4,000 attended." "These two performances netted the church $1300 in money," remembered Jones.

The wild encores at the Municipal Auditorium caused the Celestial Choir to sing spirituals from its repertoire to placate the audience at the end of performances. While one of these spirituals, "Swing Low, Sweet Chariot," was being sung softly by the choir, a huge white chariot carrying one of the Pilgrims glided across the stage to bring the performance to a spectacular close. Eventually these added spirituals became a permanent part of the play, creating what was in effect a second climax, after the slaying of Satan.

Convinced of the play's potential, Nellie Davis, had taken the lead in expanding it. After the first performance, Davis had fleshed out the various dramatic parts, and by adding ten characters to Lula Jones's original ten Pilgrims, she had broadened the array of human predicaments portrayed. An episode in which a Rich Man begrudges help to a Widow who is accompanied by a Blind Girl and some Orphans was Davis's idea. Davis also changed the original Wayward Girl from a frivolous character to a "dissolute drunkard."

Other changes appeared as the play evolved during the first year. The group of characters that had been called Pilgrims to Heaven were given specific named roles such as the Pilgrim to Zion, the Pilgrim of Sorrow, the Pilgrim of the Cross, and so on. The length of the play increased from forty-five minutes to one and a half hours. The sequence of Pilgrims was also changed so that the Soldier replaced the Drunkard as the last Pilgrim to appear. This rearrangement allowed the Soldier to kill the devil, thus bringing the play to a more fitting climax.

After the initial success of *Heaven Bound* many churches around Georgia began asking for the script of the spectacular new play. Bedazzled by this overwhelming demand, Davis, along with the pastor, B. G. Dawson, turned down the requests. So popular and so effective was the play as a fund-raiser that other churches went ahead performing it, without permission. Even some of Big Bethel's neighboring black churches attempted to "steal" the play. Within blocks of Big Bethel, Mt. Zion Church and Wheat Street Church were two of the culprits. Another church, Bethlehem, in the nearby Summerhill neighborhood, also put on Big Bethel's play. But Martha Garner, an angry Big Bethelite who went to investigate discounted the unauthorized version: "All the little churches tried it but they didn't have no people."

THE FOURTH WARD AND AUBURN AVENUE—ATLANTA'S HARLEM

Although Harlem was commonly thought of as the center of artistic expression among blacks, signs of the Harlem Renaissance were evident in such black urban communities as Detroit, Washington, D.C., Houston, Charlotte, and Chicago's South Side. The movement also made its mark in Atlanta's old Fourth Ward. Although not as large as Harlem, the Fourth Ward was a mature community with an active black intelligentsia and a commercial center that was a showcase of black entrepreneurship in the South. All the black neighborhoods of the Fourth Ward, especially the Yonge Street, Howell Street, and Houston Street neighborhoods, contributed to the thriving commerce and rich folklore of Auburn Avenue.

This environment was not only the social frame of reference for the play's authors but also a stable platform from which to offer *Heaven Bound* to the world. A stroll along Auburn revealed tailors, barbers, plumbers, and other craftsmen hard at work in their shops and parlors. A few steps from the church were banks, insurance companies, and the ever-present undertakers. Restaurants, from the white-linen variety to soul food cafes, abounded along the strip. Across the street from the church was Yates and Milton's drugstore, and a few steps beyond that, a theater offered moving pictures and live entertainment. Although black publications such as the *Pittsburgh Courier* brought news about noted black entertainers and black artists in the North, Auburn Avenue had its own daily journal, the *Atlanta Daily World.* In 1930, more than 120 businesses and 39 professionals were established along the Auburn Avenue strip.

In addition to the businesses in the vicinity, a library and schools at all levels flourished as symbols of the powerful new literacy. Just a few blocks from Big Bethel was Morris Brown College, which had been founded in Old Bethel in 1881. Another school, right across the street from Big Bethel, was the Atlanta School of Social Work, which eventually became a part of Atlanta University.

Because the traditional southern theater was reserved exclusively for whites, the black churches were fertile ground for black artistic expression. Several black amateur playwrights emerged in the Auburn Avenue churches. Plays celebrating Christmas and Easter, as well as historical skits and dramas written to mark special events in the churches, were commonplace. Although the plays were usually small projects, they were sometimes huge successes in Atlanta. Julia Borders, the scholarly wife of the new pastor of nearby Wheat Street Church, wrote a drama in 1939 depicting the Crucifixion and the Resurrection. The drama included a cast of two hundred people. Later, in 1945, Borders captured Wheat Street's history in a play entitled, *Seventy-five Years upon This Rock,* which drew thousands of people to its debut in Wheat Street's large sanctuary.

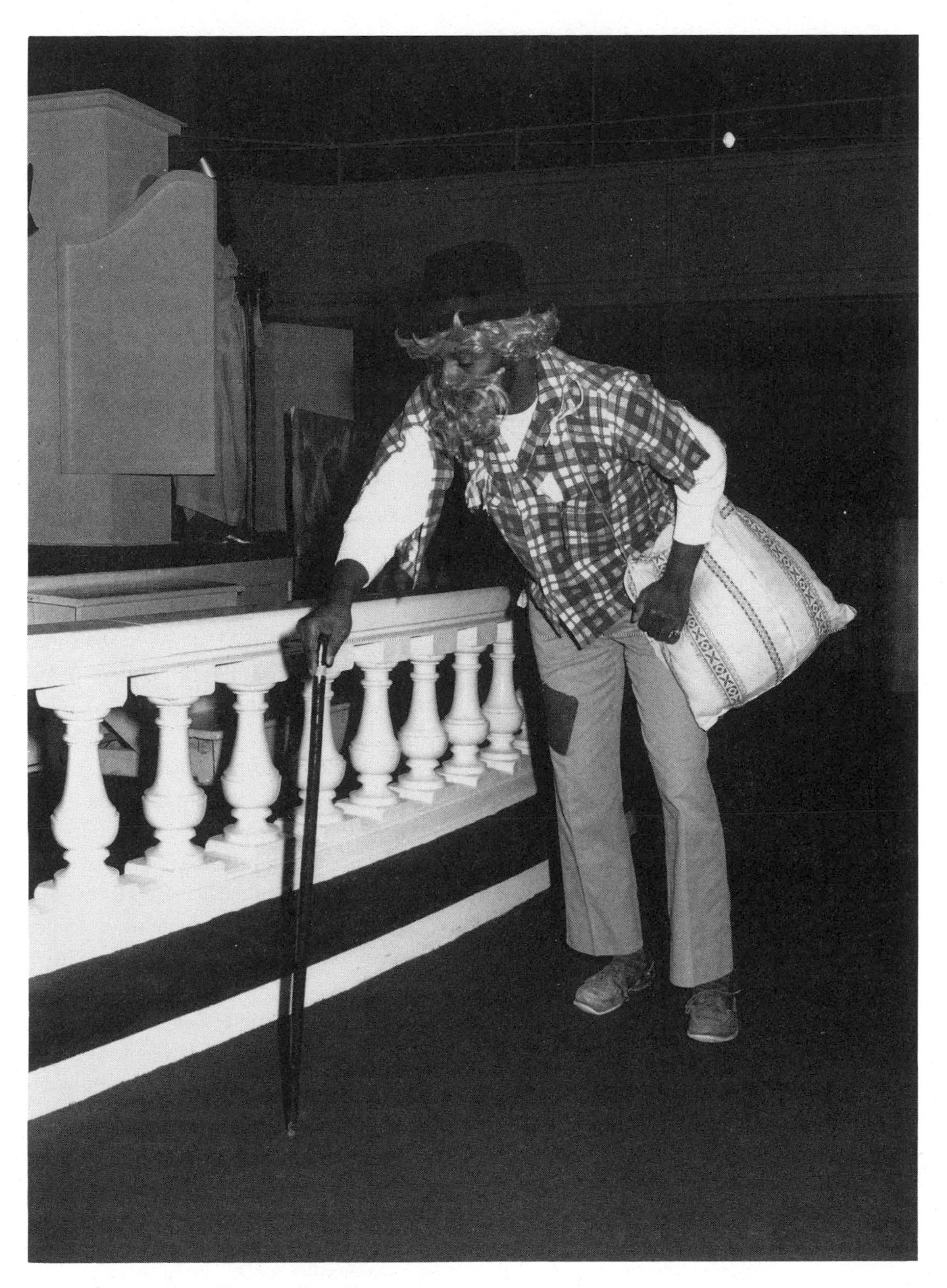

Robert Mason as the Wayworn Traveller.

BIG BETHEL, A GOOD HOME FOR THE PLAY

Because Bethel Church was situated at the center of Atlanta's black community, it was appropriate for *Heaven Bound* to settle there and become an Atlanta tradition. Big Bethel's history, triumphs, and defeats mirrored the history of black people. Its congregation had been in the forefront of the drive toward Negro literacy that eventually lead to the Harlem Renaissance. Bethel Tabernacle had been the scene of the first post–Civil War school for blacks in Atlanta, and Old Bethel had been the birthplace of a liberal arts college.

The characteristics of the congregation were good for the play. Its members were hometown folks, most of whom lived right in the neighborhood. They mingled freely with the preachers, merchants, pundits, and derelicts along Auburn Avenue. Everybody knew everybody. For the next thirty years or so, Bethel remained a church of the neighborhood, a church where people absorbed values, grew up, got married, reared their children, and died.

Although a few of Big Bethel's members lived the privileged life, most of those who produced and performed the first *Heaven Bound* were a common lot. Thousands of black men and 90 percent of all black women employed in Atlanta in 1930 worked as domestics for whites. Most of the first Angels, Pilgrims, and members of the Celestial Choir were maids, butlers, or yardmen. Their meager means notwithstanding, they had an abundance of dignity and pride. They got along, therefore, just fine. A few of the first players enjoyed higher earnings from employment as waiters and bellhops in the local hotels and restaurants. These workers, like the redcaps in Atlanta's train station, earned generous tips. The play's Satan, George Pullum, held the kind of job most prized by local black men without much formal education. As a mail clerk for one of Atlanta's railway companies, Pullum was a "railroad man." But whatever their station in life, these resourceful people proudly stepped forward, ready to lend their hands and voices to the new play. Some even became stars in the drama, projecting into their roles all the color and authenticity of their daily struggle.

Just as important as the hardworking adults who created and starred in the play were Big Bethel's youth. Coming from such nearby black neighborhoods as Pittsburgh, Summerhill, and Dark Town, large groups of children in the early 1930s walked to the church on Sunday mornings. Their parents, usually stern disciplinarians, walked behind them, making sure that none veered astray. "We knew how to have fun," recalled Lena Dean Douglas, one of the church's teenagers at that time. "We would meet for ice cream sodas at Yates and Milton's. . . . It was our choir, the Junior Choir, that made the first crepe paper wings for the play's angels." It was also Douglas who, as a child herself, lined up other children in the neighborhood to march around in the streets singing "When the Saints Go Marching In." It was the children's own rendition of *Heaven Bound.*

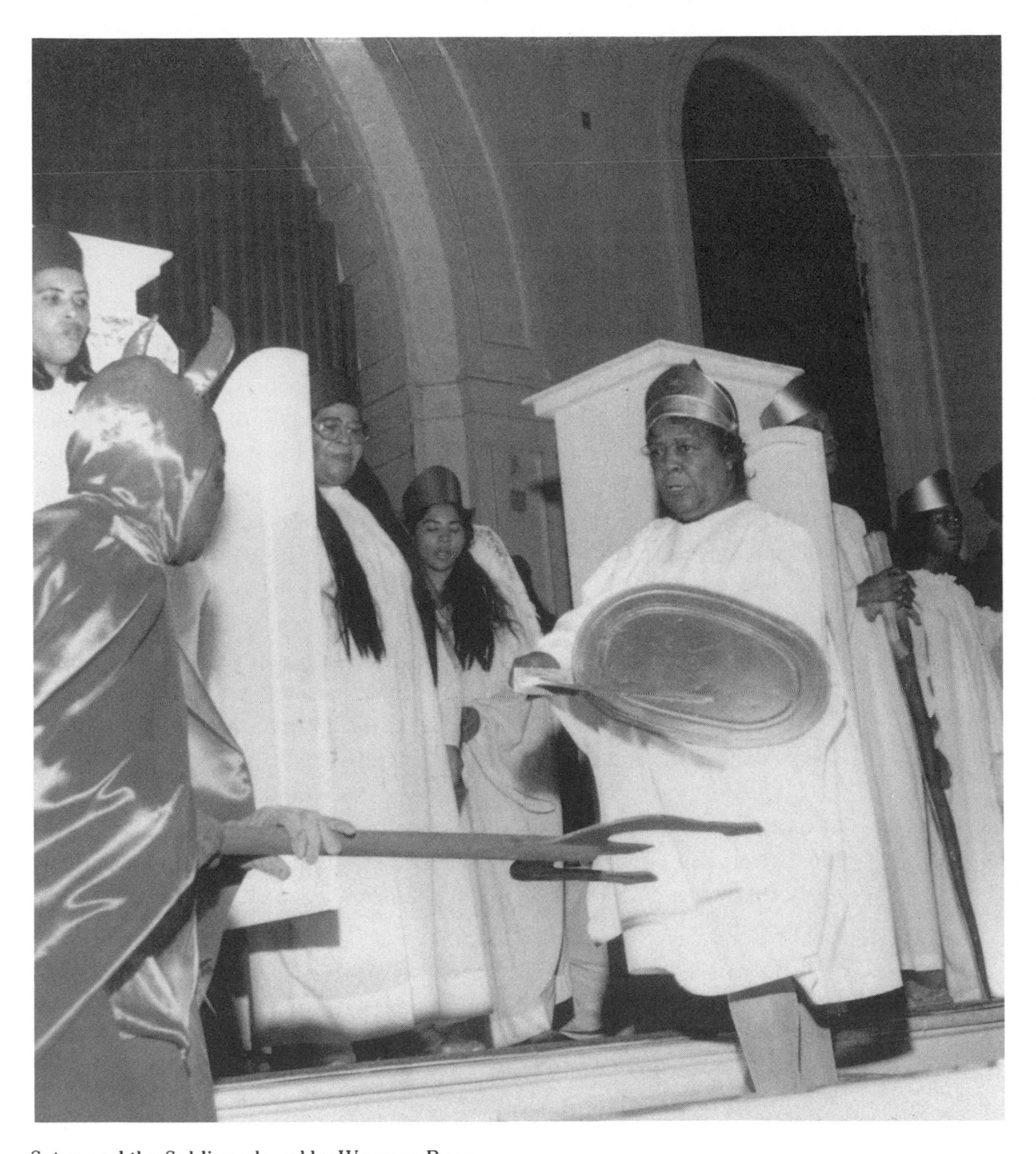

Satan and the Soldier, played by Waymon Bray.

All the youngsters later groomed for the play were members of the Junior Choir. A group meticulously well trained by the bishop's daughter, Sujette Fountain, the Junior Choir sang from the church's balcony on Sunday mornings. As they turned eighteen, members of the Junior Choir became eligible to join the adult choirs. These young people watched closely and waited patiently for their turn at stardom. Eventually, many were called on to participate in the play.

One young lady in the Junior Choir, whose life became a chapter in the history of the play, was Waymon Jennings Bray. Destined to become the Soldier in the Army of the Lord, Bray, like Sarah Williams and Nellie Davis, who preceded her in the role, was a strong soprano. Her voice had a birdlike quality that was a favorite with *Heaven Bound* audiences. The character of the Soldier, which she portrayed for fifty years, was apt for her. A fateful accident would leave her a young widow, with three small children and limited means. Nevertheless, she performed her role in the play with all the force, intensity, and conviction with which she faced life. With helmet, sword, and shield, Bray met old Satan head-on in the church's aisles. In the heated clashes, she sang loudly the lyrics "You have to fight sometimes" from her assigned solo, "I'm a Soldier." And fight she did, in the play as well as in real life. Eventually, Bray saw each of her children graduate from college and one of them from law school.

Others in the Junior Choir also became luminaries in the church play. Charlie Zanders and Raymond Dean, the leaders of a benevolent gang of boys called the Eight Musketeers, became two of the best Gamblers *Heaven Bound* ever had. Coy Jones, another Junior Choir teenager, turned out to be an irrepressible Striver, and Harriette Baynes was a celestial pianist for more than forty years. Henry Jones Jr., Viola Cleveland, Addison Campbell, Charlie Bishop, and others in the talented, robust group of youngsters were loyal to the play until their deaths.

The stability of Big Bethel's congregation helped preserve the play and pass it along to the church members. Many features of *Heaven Bound,* especially the folklike style and dramatic interpretation so popular with audiences, could not be put in writing. But because the membership was stable and the presentations of *Heaven Bound* so frequent, the play's unwritten detail was in no danger of being lost and could pass from one Big Bethel generation to the next. Over the years, this process based on firsthand observation and oral transmission brought the play near to perfection. Besides, most of the church's members preferred the oral method of passing along the uncopyrighted play. It was the best way to keep other churches from "stealing" it.

Because *Heaven Bound* was peculiar to Big Bethel Church, other churches trying to duplicate it failed. Their congregations lacked the talent and commitment necessary to bring the play to life and to perpetuate it. They also lacked

The cast inside the pulpit Heaven, 1985.

another advantage enjoyed by Big Bethel: the design of its sanctuary. The high arched auditorium had a heavenly air not present in many other churches. The chancel met most peoples' mental image of Heaven (during performances of the play, the elevated choir loft served as the pinnacle of Heaven). Rising majestically behind the choir loft was a tremendous white arch lined with lights. Vertically arranged within the arch was the panel of golden pipes of the Moller organ. In front of the arch and choir loft, extending outward, was a pulpit-in-the-round, where the Pilgrims entered Heaven through the Pearly Gates. An elegant white altar rail made a semicircle around the pulpit and met the imposing arch at its base. It was all a dramatic backdrop for a religious play and a Heaven that could be "stolen" only with the architecture itself.

The Human Side of Angels

I want the church, the choir to continue to play it, but I just wanted a little royalty.
—Lula Byrd Jones

I gave her [Lula Jones] credit for bringing the idea but I contend that I was entitled to credit for the authorship of the play.—Nellie Davis

WHOSE PLAY? WHOSE MONEY?

The Depression was deepening and times were hard. The huge mortgage on the rebuilt church was unbearable. The church had prayed and waited for divine intervention, and *Heaven Bound* appeared with its extraordinary drawing power. Atlanta newspapers, both white and black, described the enormous crowds attracted to the nine performances presented during the first year. From those performances, the church had profited by "several thousand dollars."

In its second year, the play continued to evolve. Lula Jones's original cast of characters had doubled, and the play was twice as long. Big Bethel presented the play as many times during the first four months of 1931 as it had in all the previous year. Again, to accommodate the crowds, the play was moved from the church several times and presented in large public auditoriums.

During its second year, the play toured the state, stopping at places where others watched and made plans to duplicate it. Before long, several theater companies on college campuses and in churches around the Southeast were also presenting the new *Heaven Bound.* The *Atlanta Daily World* reported performances of the play by groups in Birmingham, Orlando, and Memphis. *Time* magazine even reported a performance scheduled to open in Philadelphia in September 1931. The hype and the hoopla, the huge audiences, and the national publicity all pointed to the great and tantalizing promise of money.

Little did anyone imagine that only a year after *Heaven Bound* made its debut, the authors of this sacred play and the officials of Bethel Church would be embroiled in a series of internecine legal skirmishes focused on determining who was the true author of the play. Published reports, based on rumor rather than fact, were already adding to the confusion by giving the credit to an unnamed laundry worker in Jacksonville, Florida. The woman, who was said to have dreamt the *Heaven Bound* idea after a strenuous day's work "over her steaming suds," was, of course, a complete fiction. It was actually Big Bethel's own Lula Jones who presented the idea of the play to the church. And it was Jones who added details to it and starred in it. But others in the choir added to Jones's idea. The person who added the most to the development of *Heaven Bound,* Nellie Davis, found herself competing with Jones for the coveted title of author.

It appeared that there were two *Heaven Bound*s, not two plays but two versions of the same play. Jones and Davis each had her own manuscript of the play, complete with descriptions of the set and directions for each role. Jones claimed to have written her version in October and November 1929. Davis pinpointed the time of her written version as January 1930. Although the Jones version was never used in presenting the play and was seen by almost nobody other than herself, Jones claimed that it was indeed the original version of the play and that it was written before Davis's version.

The two versions were similar. Not only the interstitial readings but the characters and the sequence of their appearance were alike. The only difference between the two manuscripts was the language employed. When asked to explain the similarities of the two versions, Jones maintained that she had "dictated" her characters to Davis. If this was true, it meant that Davis was Jones's agent and had written ideas that actually belonged to Jones. Davis counterclaimed that it was Jones and her cohorts who were seeking undeserved credit for ideas that did not belong to them. Furthermore, contended Davis, it was Jones's coworker at the laundry, not Jones, who had originated the idea in the first place. Although each author claimed steadfastly that she had not seen nor copied from the manuscript written by the other, Davis accused Jones of stealing the Davis manuscript and changing it slightly to look like a different version.

It was a lesson in human nature. Inside Big Bethel, everyone's ego was swollen because of the popularity of the great play that both Davis and Jones laid claim to. The stakes were high. The crowds demanding to see the play brought thousands of dollars to the church's empty coffers. And awaiting the person who could be identified as the author of the play were fame, clout, and the limelight. The lure of this once-in-a-lifetime chance for fortune and fame was too powerful, and the parties involved were reduced to petty bickering, swearing, and personal insults. These "angels," as though fallen out of

Heaven, had succumbed to the sweet taste of fame, proving one thing beyond all doubt—they were still human.

It was a full-scale legal fight. Nellie Davis was the defendant, along with Big Bethel Church. Educated, twenty-nine years old, and a relative newcomer to the choir, Davis carried the banner of the church's up-and-coming youth. The pastor and the trustees, all successful, influential people in the church and in the community, stood with Davis, giving her the support of the "in-crowd." In contrast, Lula Jones worked at a laundry and was the senior member of the choir, representing the beleaguered older choir members. Only those with the courage of their conviction stood with Jones on what was the unpopular side of the case.

The uncertainty about the legal ownership of the play had an effect lasting far beyond the trial. As if their copyright had already been officially recognized, officials of Big Bethel started requiring other churches to get permission before presenting the play. Eventually no church but Big Bethel performed the play. The Scroll Reading was kept out of the public eye, and the long years of "hoarding" the play began.

THE JONESES GET A COPYRIGHT

After seeing the first performance of *Heaven Bound,* Pastor Dawson asked one of the play's Angels, Ruby Lloyd, to tell him who wrote the play. Lloyd responded by bringing Lula Jones to the pastor's study to be congratulated. Following that encounter, however, the pastor must have heard that someone else had written the play, for after the next several performances, he went before audiences and announced, without mentioning Jones's name, that it was Nellie Davis who wrote the play. Although she objected to the pastor's actions, Jones did not object at the time.

One particular occasion, when the pastor insisted that Nellie Davis receive all the credit for creating the play, was the catalyst for a remarkable turn of events. It was a Friday night in November 1930. *Heaven Bound* was being presented at Bethel Church under the sponsorship of Atlanta's white-only Saint Mark Methodist Church. After the performance, the pastor went to the front of the church and announced that Davis was the author of the play. The following Sunday morning, an article covering the performance appeared in the *Atlanta Journal Magazine,* and only Nellie Davis was named as the author. It was the *Journal*'s omission of Lula Jones's name that caused the Joneses to break their silence, and for the next four months, Lula Jones, vying for a place in the spotlight, engaged in a series of events that set the church and the community abuzz for the next year and a half. In response to the article in the

Journal Magazine, Jones's husband, Henry, went to the Forsyth Street office of Angus Perkerson, the magazine's editor, and demanded that the newspaper print a correction. The newspaper responded, however, by printing only that Lula Jones was the "introducer" of the play, not its author.

Shortly after the dispute with the *Journal Magazine,* Lula Jones decided to register her copyright claim with the Copyright Office in Washington, D.C. Her husband engaged Ruby Lloyd, the secretary of the choir as well as a secretary with an Auburn Avenue real estate firm, to type what became known as the Jones readings for *Heaven Bound.* The typed material was then taken to the House of Murphy, an offset printing shop, and the complete package was sent to the Copyright Office, where on January 14, 1931, Lula Jones's copyright claim was registered. Under the then-prevailing law, Jones's version of the play was entitled to protection by the copyright law for twenty-eight years, plus an additional twenty-eight-year renewal period, if it was requested.

Jones and her husband published in all the local papers notices of her copyright. The notices warned potential sponsors of the play that permission from Jones would be necessary before *Heaven Bound* could be performed. These warnings soon took effect. Some local sponsors, worried about potential liability to the Joneses, refused to allow the play to be performed at their facilities. Word of the copyright protection must have spread throughout the region, for theater companies and churches in other southern cities virtually stopped presenting the play.

THE TENSION MOUNTS

Lula Jones's copyright and the warnings in the newspapers threatened to cut off the handsome profits the financially strapped church enjoyed from the play. After Jones registered her copyright, the pastor and officers of the church were hesitant to present *Heaven Bound* again. The tension mounted, and it became uncomfortable for Jones to appear at choir rehearsal:

> I did not go to rehearsal much because some of the members—Nellie was one—wanted to fuss with me. Nellie got fighting mad with me. . . . I did not have any words with the pastor. I tried to be in harmony with him. Nellie said at choir practice in my presence that we were fighting the choir, I and my husband. She said that my husband and I were digging the dirt from under the choir's feet and that if we were going to fight it she would rather we would send in our resignations and get out of the choir. That was after I had the copyright, along in January, 1931. Since then my husband and I have not had anything to do with the choir.

Before Jones registered her copyright, a performance of the play had already been scheduled for January 29, 1931. Although the performance was to be at

Big Bethel, it was being sponsored by the white-only Peachtree Road Presbyterian Church. After learning of Jones's copyright registration, Big Bethel church officials were about to call off the performance when Clifford Anderson, a lawyer from Peachtree Road Church, stepped forward. Anderson advised the officers of Bethel Church that their rights in the play were legally superior to those of Jones. Following Anderson's advice, the church went ahead with the performance.

That performance was the last in which Jones would participate. A month later, Pastor Dawson officially ousted her and her husband from the choir. Henry remembered it in detail: "Just a few days prior to the 25th of February—it was on the 25th or around the 25th [1931]—the Rev. B. G. Dawson stopped me on the street and said to me: 'Brother Jones, I will take this opportunity to serve notice that you and your wife are no longer members of the choir . . . you are fighting the church.'" Henry protested the pastor's action and questioned his authority, but the pastor snapped back, "All the way to the general conference [the denomination's highest policy making body]—you are not members of the choir any more."

THE CHURCH GOES TO COURT

A few days after being put out of the choir, Lula Jones wrote a letter in which she asked the church for 15 percent of all future proceeds from the play. She cited her registered copyright to back up her request. Adamant in their position that Jones should not get a dime from ticket sales, the church officials ignored Jones's letter and went ahead with the next performance at the Joel Chandler Harris School, a school for whites only, in Atlanta's West End neighborhood.

About a week later, in early March, Big Bethel sent its lawyer, Anderson, to Atlanta's Fulton County Superior Court, to obtain a court order restraining both Lula and Henry Jones from publishing further notices that they owned the play. The church persuaded the Georgia court that Nellie Davis was the sole author of *Heaven Bound* and that she had transferred all her rights in the play to the church, and the court issued a temporary order restraining the Joneses from making the claim of ownership. The first-round victory, therefore, went to Big Bethel.

From this point, however, the lawyers set sail on a sea of legal theory, leaving far behind the church people and their limited understanding of copyright law. Jones seemed to believe, in error, that because she had the idea for *Heaven Bound* and introduced it to Big Bethel Church she was entitled to the copyright. Nellie Davis and the church officers also misunderstood the law, believing that Davis's position as the official chorister of the choir and coordinator of the play somehow entitled her to a special claim to the play. Neither party seemed to understand that for one or the other to qualify for the rights to *Heaven Bound* at least two requirements had to be filled. First, a written version of the play had to be produced. Second, that written version had to be the "original" work, the "independent creation" of the person claiming to be the "author." The only legality that everybody seemed to understand clearly was that Jones had somehow registered a copyright protected by federal law, and it was difficult to get around it by simply appealing to a Georgia court.

LULA JONES—DOWN, BUT NOT DEFEATED

Although the Georgia court's temporary restraining order against the Joneses went into effect, the proceeding was cut short before the order could become permanent. Instead of continuing to fight in the Georgia courts, the Joneses took the case to a higher court, the District Court of the United States for the Northern District of Georgia. The lawsuit, *Lula B. Jones v. David T. Howard, et al.,* was filed on March 14, 1931. Jones maintained that Nellie Davis and the trustees of Bethel Church had violated Jones's copyright and had failed to comply with her request for royalties.

Federal marshals served subpoenas on Cornelius King and David T. Howard, two of the church officers. Howard, a former slave, who was fourteen years old at Emancipation, had been a member of the congregation since the days of Bethel Tabernacle. A successful undertaker in the Auburn Avenue community, Howard often lent his own money to the financially strapped church. Like Howard, Cornelius King had been born a slave, but by 1931 he was a successful real estate broker with an office on Auburn Avenue. As chairman of the church's board of trustees, King was primarily responsible for keeping track of *Heaven Bound*'s revenues and expenses.

The lawyers involved in the lawsuit were Granger Hansell and E. Smythe Gambrell, names attached to prestigious Atlanta law firms. In one of the stately wainscoted courtrooms of the old federal courthouse on Forsyth Street, Judge Marvin Underwood presided. During the fourteen months he deliberated, Underwood allowed both Big Bethel Church and Lula Jones to enjoy some privileges of ownership. Each could present, or authorize others to present, the play, although neither could interfere with performances given or authorized by the other. During the many months of litigation, therefore, *Heaven Bound* continued to be presented by Big Bethel in its own sanctuary as well as at other churches and schools. Although it was not known whether their copyright would be restored, the Joneses seemed to claim a small victory in this opening round in federal court. The order of the Georgia court was nullified when the federal court agreed to hear the case, and the Joneses, like the church officials, could again authorize performances of the play, at least while the judge was making up his mind.

JONES AND HER WITNESSES

To show Judge Underwood that her copyright had been infringed, Jones enlisted some impressive witnesses—staunch Big Bethelites of solid piety. Like Jones most of them had been members of the church and choir since the early 1900s. They believed in Lula Jones, and they believed that right was on their side. They gave to Jones's case the strength and credibility of their character.

One by one, they spoke up, even if it meant going against the pastor and church officers. Josephine Singleton Bigsby, who played the Mother in Heaven, stepped forward. She was the former chorister of Choir Number One and the wife of one of the church's former pastors. Joining Bigsby on Jones's behalf were others—A. D. Hodges, a painter who played the Reformed Drunkard; M. T. Wyche, a barber at Atlanta's Terminal Station; and Wesley Clark, a Pullman car porter who was one of the original Pilgrims. These witnesses described in detail that particular night at choir rehearsal when Lula Jones first mentioned the play to the choir. Still other witnesses, like Jones's niece Mary Brinkley, tried to help prove that Jones's version of the play had been written two months before the Davis version surfaced.

Ruby Lloyd was a particularly credible witness for Jones: "I have been in almost all of the performances of the play. . . . Lula Jones brought the original play to the church. I don't see how anybody could deny that. . . . I have been pretty regular at the rehearsals. I was there at the organization [of *Heaven Bound*] right in the beginning. I have never heard Nellie Davis say that she wrote the play or was responsible for it. The only part she was responsible for was some readings."

Of course Henry Jones testified on behalf of his wife. While the church's lawyers took great pains to portray Lula Jones as an undereducated woman, with little ability, if any, to write a play, they portrayed Henry as a meddlesome, quarrelsome mastermind working in the background in support of his wife's position. Each of the fifteen or so witnesses on the side of Davis and the church was coached to recite the same litany of criticism about Henry in their sworn affidavits: "[t]hat said Lula Jones never intended to claim credit for the authorship of said play but that she was instigated thereto by her husband, Henry Jones, who stated . . . that said Lula Jones had as much brains as Nellie Davis and that she ought to write said play, send it to Washington and have it copyrighted."

In what seemed to be a downturn in the case, Henry testified that his wife kept her written version of the play in her trunk and that he did not see it until May 1930, six months after the Davis version was written. Although Henry was Lula Jones's most ardent supporter, his testimony was of no help to his wife's case.

Lula Jones's copyright infringement lawsuit was, by its very nature, a serious indictment of the character of Nellie Davis and the church's officers. The lawsuit was, in effect, an accusation of theft. Once on the witness stand, however, Jones did not seem inclined to accuse anyone. Her testimony was surprisingly mild, as she simply tried to hold on to some of the credit the church and its lawyers tried so desperately to give to her coworker at the laundry, Belle Thomas, and Nellie Davis.

Jones seemed perfectly willing to give Thomas and Davis the credit she felt they deserved, but nothing amounting to authorship of the play. That she reserved for herself. Explaining vigorously that Thomas had not given her the original idea for *Heaven Bound* but had only served as a sounding board and a source of some minor suggestions, Jones testified, "Belle Thomas told me we could have the angels in it and . . . the wayward girl or the devil one. . . . She spoke about some songs we might sing and we didn't sing the songs she suggested, we got some other songs I thought more appropriate." Regarding Davis's contribution to the play, Jones said, "I did not write the readings that they read in the play. . . . Nellie Davis used her readings. The readings are based on the ideas that I took there. They are the same thing the drama is." Comparing her version with the Davis version, Jones readily admitted, "I noticed them being similar. . . ." Then Jones attempted to explain how her ideas and contributions could be so similar to those of Davis: "I trained the choir to start with. . . . After we had played it the first time Nellie Davis trained them. . . . Nellie Davis added some pieces to it. . . . I thought it would be all right." But Jones stopped short of accusing Davis of an improper duplication. In what must have been a detour quite startling to Jones's lawyers, Jones seemed even to protect Davis, by testifying, "She didn't see mine and I didn't see hers."

NELLIE DAVIS—IN HER OWN DEFENSE

Pastor Dawson, the official spokesperson for the church, was so obviously biased in giving Davis all the credit that she could not bring herself to receive it all. Even Davis had to admit that Dawson knew only what he had been told by others. Besides, the church's rumor mill had already ascribed to the pastor some ulterior motives explaining his enthusiasm for the pretty young chorister.

Davis took the witness stand with wit, intellect, and a sharp tongue. She did not hesitate to denigrate Jones's witnesses. When asked whether she knew Ruby Lloyd, Davis replied, "I wouldn't vouch for her truthfulness. . . . I understand she helped them write that jump the rope that they sent to Washington." Davis also accused Jones and her witnesses of a "surreptitious" plot to steal the Davis manuscript. Davis implied that John Bigsby had gone to the printing shop where the Davis readings were being printed and tricked the printer into giving him one of the copies. Davis speculated that it was this copy of her play that had found its way into the hands of Lula Jones and from which Jones had written "her play, making only slight variations. . . ."

Even though she freely gave Jones credit for "introducing" the idea of the play, Davis was much less generous in assigning credit for its authorship: "I got the idea from Lula Jones. . . . I lay no claim to the originality of the idea, but I do lay claim to the development of that idea. . . . I always turned and gave her [Jones] credit for getting me to put it on."

Trying to help Judge Underwood understand exactly how her ideas became intertwined with those of Lula Jones, Davis testified, "[T] his thing has been built up. . . . Lula Jones told me that there were pilgrims on the way to heaven singing songs that had to do with heaven, and she said there would be Satan in the play, and he would tempt these pilgrims, and a wayward girl who was lost and had to go to hell, and a drunkard. . . . Lula Jones never did anything but give me the original idea of it, and I have developed it myself, she just gave us the skeleton of it." Although Davis argued that Jones gave her only "the skeleton of it," she seemed willing to concede at least half of the play to Jones. Admitting that Jones's version of the play initially included ten pilgrims and lasted only forty-five minutes, Davis explained that she, herself, had added ten pilgrims, doubling the length of the play.

DECISION

Judge Underwood's decision was, no doubt, a crushing defeat for Lula Jones. Underwood said, "I find that the complainant [Lula Jones] got the general theme and most, if not all, of the characters . . . from her co-worker at the laundry [Belle Thomas] . . . that from this nucleus, and the additions suggested by the chorister [Nellie Davis], the choir, including complainant [Lula Jones], the play developed." In his decision, Judge Underwood suggested that the final version of *Heaven Bound* was indeed an "original" work that might be copyrighted. He seemed to feel, however, that because several people had contributed ideas to the final product, no single person could claim the whole work.

The possibility was left open that the church—which was the common ground where all parties met and made their contributions—might rightfully claim the entire play and obtain a copyright. That is, if Belle Thomas did not show up to claim a copyright of her own. She never did.

CLOSING THE WOUND

Curiously, the newspapers and magazines seemed unaware of the trial. At the same time that *Time* magazine was printing that the play "originated in the fervent head of Lula Jones," the federal judge was reaching a different conclusion. It was also surprising how quickly the whole affair was hushed up around the church. The twenty-five church members who had testified during the trial agreed to keep silent. Even Lula Jones's stepchildren, Thelma Jones Belt and Henry Jones Jr., chose not to remember the unpleasant details of the trial; they remembered only the embarrassment. Because the newspapers had "missed" the trial and the church people involved were reluctant to talk about it, any gossip that might have stemmed from the lawsuit was squelched. Silence fell over the church as if to bury the shame of the conflict.

It was not just embarrassment that kept Big Bethel silent about the copyright fight. Because no one person was granted the protection of copyright, the play appeared to be freely available to other churches and theater companies. So in their silence, the parishioners pretended that the church controlled the copyright in *Heaven Bound.* Nobody in the church would talk about a Scroll Reading, a libretto, or song sheets. The play was taught only to members of Big Bethel and to out-of-town churches approved by Nellie Davis.

Occasional performances of *Heaven Bound* were reported in places as far away as Washington, D.C., New York City, and Richmond, Virginia. These versions of the play were probably adapted from the memories of people who had seen it at Big Bethel or at one of the churches whose choirs were trained by Davis to perform it. But after a while, and for the next fifty years, fewer and fewer churches attempted to duplicate the play. Even journalists and scholars probing the play's origins, and young Bethelites trying to piece together their history, were shut off from information about the source of the play.

After the dramatic lawsuit, the bishop of the Georgia district assigned Pastor Dawson to another church. Finding no support in the legal system, Lula Jones, hurt, aging, and disavowed, made no further attempt to establish her ownership of the play. She disappeared from the public eye and lived out her days in the church in quiet oblivion.

The Great Depression: Golden Years for *Heaven Bound*

A TIME OF CHALLENGE

By 1932, while the church struggled with its heavy financial burden, the Depression tightened its grip. Something was wrong, terribly wrong, with the economy. The circulation of money, like the rolling good times of the 1920s, had come to a screeching halt. Several families joining Bethel Church at that time, including the Mapps, the Maceo Turners, and the Braswells, had been driven from the rural farmlands by the devastation of the boll weevil, the drought, the lack of credit, and the futility of sharecropping.

Migrants moving to the cities sometimes found the situations there even more dire than the ones they had left. By 1935, 60 percent of Atlanta's employable blacks were on relief. Success was not "just around the corner," as President Hoover had promised while he was in office. The times were trying. People had to pray hard and hold tight to their faith, often clinging to thoughts of "a better place" as a means of escape. The prospect of Heaven along with President Roosevelt's soothing promises of recovery offered some solace to the many people whose earthly horizons were dimmed to the point of hopelessness.

By the early part of the 1930s, time had made some changes among the *Heaven Bound* regulars. Brother Matthews, who had played Saint Peter, "crossed the river" after a long and fascinating life. Also passing off the scene were the church officers Cornelius King and David T. Howard, who had tended the financial and legal affairs of the church and the play. A major change also occurred in the cast: George Pullum had become too fat for the strenuous role of Satan and was replaced in 1933 by a young high school professor by the name of Henry James Furlow. Pullum was given the more accommodating role of the Wayworn Traveller.

Although the Depression and the resulting despair had all but paralyzed the country, God seemed to smile on *Heaven Bound,* and this folk drama was about to see its finest hour. Nellie Davis, and the new Satan, H. J. Furlow, were both young, talented, dedicated, and strong. They would prove absolutely formidable in combination. The Bethel choirs were at their best. Both Number One

The Wayworn Traveller played by George Pullum, who was the first Satan.

and Number Two were cohesive groups, replenished by fresh talent moving up from the Junior Choir. The meticulous Davis was a fine choral conductor who relentlessly drilled her beloved Number One to perfection. Number Two, under the direction of Helen Massey, was building quite a reputation for itself, singing the spirituals in concerts around town.

Charity Collins Miles, who was one of the few black registered nurses in her day and played the Widow in *Heaven Bound,* kept a scrapbook showing the many places around the city where the choirs put on miniconcerts featuring the spirituals. The old military hospital (called Base 48), the landmark Five Points intersection in downtown Atlanta, the Lullwater Park, and even the Salvation Army school were among the stops. The choirs also sang at various private gatherings and were heard on the WSB radio station. No church in Atlanta was better known than Big Bethel for the fine music of its choirs. And no church group was more ready, willing, and able to meet the challenge ahead than the choirs of Big Bethel.

MONEY AND MORALE

During the Depression, only eleven hundred of the church's three thousand members paid money into the church's treasury, and most of these paying members were unskilled laborers and domestic workers at the bottom of the wage scale. The economic base of the church's membership was too weak to support Big Bethel's enormous mortgage. The monthly mortgage payment of $650 swallowed up the nickels, dimes, and quarters that clinked into the Sunday morning offering plates.

In 1934, after Pastor Dawson and his two short-term successors were gone, Big Bethel received one of her greatest pastors—Dewitt Talmadge Babcock, known as the Little Giant. Babcock came into a distressed situation. Regular maintenance and repairs at the church had been left undone. And Babcock went for weeks without pay. But he proved equal to the challenge of the overhanging debt and adopted as his motto "It can be done!"

Under Babcock, as new sources of income were sought, all types of fundraising rallies were put to the test. Big Bethel's great auxiliary boards were encouraged to raise money from whatever sources they could find and by whatever means. Appeals continued to go out from the church to government officials and to the "white friends" in whose kitchens many of the church's members worked.

Although *Heaven Bound* had its work cut out for it for the remainder of the decade, it had already proved itself ready for the challenge. Not only did the play boost morale and offer fresh hope to the thousands of Atlantans who

Dewitt Talmadge Babcock with his officers.

BIG BETHEL
A.M.E. CHURCH

flocked to see it, it inspired people from other parts of the world as well. At a convention of the World Ecumenical Council in October 1931 more than 6,500 prelates and ministers from all corners of the globe had filled the Atlanta Municipal Auditorium to see the great play.

The reputation of the choirs and the tremendous appeal of *Heaven Bound* made the play the centerpiece of Pastor Babcock's new financial plan for the debt-ridden church. Even though the play continued to raise large sums of money, its money-making potential had not yet been fully exploited. If ticket prices had been increased, the church's debt could have been wiped out. But church officers viewed *Heaven Bound* as a ministry, the price for which could not be too high, even though some wealthy whites were willing to pay higher prices to reserve for their friends whole blocks of seats in the church, and even though performances filled the church to capacity. Because the nickels and dimes charged for admission hardly brought in more than $100 for a single performance, many performances had to be given. The 1930s, therefore, were the busiest ever for the play.

The copyright litigation of 1931–32 had caused other churches and would-be sponsors to back away from the play. During the Babcock years, therefore, Bethel Church was the site of most performances of *Heaven Bound* and the clearinghouse for permission to present the play elsewhere. This arrangement kept the money flowing into the church. Scores of performances continued to be presented by Big Bethel, including several for convention delegates and other large crowds at the Municipal Auditorium. It was during these years that the cast also toured extensively, playing such rural Georgia towns as Dublin, Newnan, Buford, Rome, and Marietta. The church also took the play out of state to Chattanooga, Nashville, and Lake Junaluska, North Carolina.

Heaven Bound performers such as Edna Collier, Martha Garner, Evvie Mabry, and Esther McDonald were young, energetic players during the 1930s and responded to the call when the church stepped up its *Heaven Bound* schedule, taking the play to various schools and churches, both black and white. In 1931 the play was presented by the Big Bethel choirs on thirty-seven occasions, an average of more than three performances per month. After Sunday morning worship, the choirs would hustle out of the church and into buses that took them on tour. Sometimes the tours required overnight stays, and choir members with small children or restrictive jobs could not go. Skeletal casts from the play were sometimes taken along to combine with and train larger groups in other churches. This was all done with Big Bethel's permission.

The stress of the tours sometimes caused excitement. On one of the tours, a choir member, Emma Akers, suffered a cardiac upset because of the way the tour bus—a school bus improperly used for long-distance travel—tossed her about. Quite a scare for the traveling players, Akers's problem luckily turned out to be only a case of "the palpitations." Another trip was taken one night in the path of an electric storm, which terrified the busload of *Heaven Bound* players. The revelation the choir experienced that night was, no doubt, clear and unmistakable—they simply were not homesick for their heavenly home.

THE GENIUS OF NELLIE DAVIS

The pace and success of *Heaven Bound* during the Depression were a testament to the dedication of the choirs and players. During this period, Nellie Davis also built a reputation for herself. A short woman with an engaging smile, Davis often wore two long braids crisscrossed atop her head. She was a vivacious person, described by her friend Carrie George as "always gushing."

A graduate of Atlanta University, Davis had absorbed the values of excellence and propriety that permeated that school's environment. At the age of thirty-five, she became an English professor at Atlanta's Clark College. And in what proved to be a remarkable move, she transferred the values of learning, propriety, and cultural refinement from the college environment to the folk arena of Big Bethel's *Heaven Bound*.

Nellie Davis was also a natural leader, with a unique ability to organize and inspire people to do their best. Indeed, leadership was a quality that seemed to be in her blood. Her father, the headwaiter in Atlanta's Henry Grady and Ansley hotels, had organized a secret society of local black waiters, back in the days when blacks could not join the historically white labor unions.

Although Davis continued to acknowledge Lula Jones as the woman who brought the idea for *Heaven Bound* to the choir, Davis's influence on the play was so thorough that, in the eyes of the public, she eclipsed Jones. Newspaper articles and printed programs continued to identify Davis as the author of the play, and the court's decision in the copyright lawsuit had silenced Jones's protests.

Whatever can be argued about the share of credit Davis did or did not deserve for authorship of the play, or about her motive in guiding it through its first years, the emerging theatrical genius of this woman was undeniable. She was multitalented. She played the piano, directed the Celestial Choir, and was noted for her remarkable voice that spanned several octaves from soprano to bass. Her portrayal of the dissipated Wayward Girl was a favorite with audiences and often provoked viewers to tears, confessions, and vows of self-renewal. Davis's gifts as a writer were evident in her Scroll Reading, a masterpiece that carried the action in the play and captivated its listeners with its elegant simplicity. In it, she introduced the Wayward Girl, the part she played herself: "What wayward frivolous soul cometh now to the gate of Heaven? She it is who has trod the primrose path, heeding not, caring not, as she quaffs the cup of pleasure to its dregs."

Davis showed her caliber as a director, as well. With a firm grasp of drama and human nature and of the common sphere connecting the two, she cast the various personalities in the church for roles in the play. Having grown up in the Auburn Avenue environs, she understood the folkways of the local blacks in the churches, nightclubs, and secret societies. As a dramatist, she also understood how those folkways illuminated and brought to life the character of each Pilgrim in the play.

Davis also grasped the texture of human relationships. She walked shoulder-to-shoulder with the bishops and elders of the church as well as with the ordinary folk. Loved by her students, she trained and organized them to present dramatic works at the college where she taught. She also worked well with the people in her choir. With those women in the choir who, like her, were estranged from their husbands, she organized a social club, the Merry Widows. One difficult challenge for Davis was that of keeping in harmony the various factions in the choirs. When the number of *Heaven Bound* performances increased, members of the two choirs became competitive and brought their gripes to rehearsals. But Davis kept things under control. "She was firm, but knew how to talk to people," recalled Edna Collier, an admiring Celestial Choir member. Each player selected by Davis to be a Pilgrim seemed to cherish her decision as the honor of a lifetime. "Nellie put me in the role of Guardian Angel back in the thirties and I've been there ever since," remarked Martha Garner, when she was a fifty-five-year veteran of the play. "Nellie called me one night in the fall of 1942 and asked me to take the role of the Hypocrite," recalled Daisy Payne Brown, another Davis fan.

HEAVEN BOUND "GOES THEATER"

The Federal Theatre Project (FTP) was a program of the Works Progress Administration (WPA), organized under the Roosevelt administration to provide work for an idle populace. A principal aim of the FTP was to give jobs to unemployed professional actors and technical personnel such as carpenters and electricians. Another aim was to encourage the production of regional drama.

By 1937, the Atlanta Studio Club, a group of wealthy whites, had reorganized itself in order to receive financial aid from the FTP. Its new name was the Atlanta Theatre Guild, but it was known simply as the Guild. Many years earlier, when it was still known as the Studio Club, the Guild had formed ties with the Big Bethel choirs. The club had sponsored the choirs' singing the spirituals at private estates in Atlanta's exclusive Buckhead section. Big Bethel's old policy

The entire cast in Heaven at the Atlanta Theatre.

of maintaining ties to Atlanta's wealthy white community seemed to pay off, because in 1937 the Guild, in joint sponsorship with the FTP, invited *Heaven Bound* to make its mainstream debut in a performance at the Atlanta Theatre, located downtown across from the Hurt Building near present-day Georgia State University, just a short walk from the church.

Heaven Bound was to break new ground, for during the 1930s the formal theater was exclusively white in the deep South, except for the black laborers who performed the menial tasks associated with theater productions. The church was to receive no money for its presentations at the theater—only exposure for the play. And the theater's white technical directors were to be given the opportunity to "improve" the play. The deal was struck and extensive preparations got under way.

In a sense, the play fell to the control of the whites once it reached the Atlanta Theatre. The blacks had no exposure to the formal theater and did not know much about it. So this was a time when the whites could not only patronize the black play but could put their mark on it as well.

Although Davis continued as the director of *Heaven Bound,* the white technical directors at the theater prepared to make fundamental changes in the play. Satan, the central figure played by H. J. Furlow, was stopped from talking and babbling as part of his role. Mute and animated, however, Furlow would go ahead with the role and do beautiful pantomime. The location of Life's Highway was also changed. All the action in the play was to be confined to the stage at the front of the theater, instead of the aisles, which had been used at the church. Also, Hell was put in the orchestra pit beneath the stage.

Even Heaven was to undergo some changes. With only their heads showing, the Angels were to stand behind beaverboard clouds arranged in tiers leading up to a cross centered at the top of the clouds. The cross was to be lighted whenever a new Pilgrim reached the promised land. Women, for the first time, were to be guardian angels at the Pearly Gates, thus taking posts previously reserved for such strapping men as John Calhoun, George Butler, and Waymon Edge. Davis at first resisted this change from men to women but later relented.

Another fundamental change made by the white directors was the switch from traditional hymns to spirituals. The Atlanta Theatre's art director, Julian Harris, recalled taking the position that the hymns the choir had been singing sounded "too white." About thirteen spirituals were added to the three already being sung. Such traditional hymns as "The Old Rugged Cross," "The Unclouded Day," and "How Firm a Foundation" gave way to such spirituals as "Ain't Dat Good News" and "I'm Trampin." Also, a miniconcert of spirituals was

Raymond Dean, the Gambler; Nellie Davis, the Wayward Girl; and Henry Furlow, Satan.

permanently adopted to enhance the finale and to keep the choir ready for the predictable encores.

It was not difficult to understand why the black players felt uncomfortable singing their spirituals in the "white theater." These black songs had only recently been accepted by whites as respectable music. Southern society was still segregated, and the theater was a strange new place for the pioneering black players. Moving away from the music that had worked so well for the play in the past seemed risky.

Some of the choir members, moreover, did not like the changes the white directors were making and were loathe to see *Heaven Bound* "go theater," where *The Green Pastures* and other religious plays had begun. The commercial emphasis of the theater, they thought, would rob the play of its power as a ministry. Besides, several of the players looked on the vastly different stage setting and the new image given *Heaven Bound* at the Atlanta Theatre as markedly inferior to the Big Bethel sanctuary.

THE ZENITH

With the power of 138 voices, the play opened to capacity crowds at the Atlanta Theatre on August 10, 1937. What was to have been a three-day run was extended throughout the week to accommodate the turn-away crowds. The blacks who piled in to see the play could not be seated on the main floor with the whites but were seated in the gallery instead. This particular restriction on the blacks—confinement to the gallery—must have been the height of all irony for those players who knew their A.M.E. history. The same restriction, enforced a hundred and fifty years earlier in a white Philadelphia church, had ignited the protest that gave birth to the African Methodist Episcopal Church.

At any rate, the crowd at the Atlanta Theatre burst into an unexpected excitement not long after the curtain rose. An Angel, Louise Taylor, had fallen twenty feet from a newly constructed Heaven, "knocking down a spotlight and losing a tooth in the decent. She had grown faint from the heat of the many light bulbs used [for] heavenly light," reported the *Atlanta Journal Magazine*.

Davis, who had been directing from a left-stage box, confessed that she was one of those who screamed when Taylor plunged. Davis had rushed to the stage, colliding in the process with Satan, who was rushing up from Hell's Den. In the split second that brought Davis to her senses, she remembered Satan saying to her, "Nellie, the show must go on." After a few moments, the show resumed with "the tinkle of a piano and the soft chant of voices." The curtain again rose, this time to thunderous sustained applause.

Critical acclaim was lavish. The artistic achievements of the play, accord-

The Soldier, played by Waymon Bray, and Satan on the steps of Heaven at the Atlanta Theatre.

ing to the reviews, soared to unprecedented heights. In the *Atlanta Journal Magazine* Medora Field Perkerson raved over the performance, calling it "a natural from its beginning . . . on its way to becoming a classic, for it is native folk drama, rising out of the lives and the soul of a race."

The *Atlanta Constitution* called it "the most elaborate production of 'Heaven Bound' ever staged . . . representing one of the most ambitious efforts by the Atlanta Federal Theater." The black newspaper, the *Atlanta Daily World,* reported that "the capacity crowd was spontaneous from beginning to end."

The *Journal* described the various acts of each Pilgrim as "interpretations eloquent of an innate gift for mimicry and pantomime on the part of the actors." So moved was Mozelle Horton, who covered the performance for the *Constitution,* that she wrote, "I would like to give special mention to all the characters of the cast if space permitted."

Some of the players were outstanding and left a distinct impression on the viewers. Nellie Davis had played the role of the drunken Wayward Girl so convincingly that after the play people wondered out loud whether Davis drank alcoholic beverages in real life. She did not. And H. J. Furlow, as Satan, certainly carved out for himself a permanent place in *Heaven Bound*'s hall of fame. Contrasting with the deadly serious message of the play was what the *Journal* called a "transcendental humor which . . . makes Satan the star of the performance." The paper continued, "His act is all pure pantomime . . . pantomime at its humorous best, which is consummate acting." The *Constitution* billed Furlow's performance "as fine a piece of acting as one could ask with an exceptionally fine chorus in the background."

The spirituals also made an impression on the new fans. "The large choir sang naturally well the spirituals. . . . These Negroes' voices blend with marvelous harmony that has a tone color peculiarly all its own, and inherent of the race." . . . "The three spirituals at the end of the play were sung with as much beauty as I have ever heard spirituals sung," reported Mozelle Horton of the *Constitution*.

Perhaps it was the shortsightedness of their youth or the sweet taste of fame that made the young *Heaven Bound* stars proceed without understudies for their roles. But the risks were overshadowed by the result. The vast number of performances and the concentrated training had brought the natural talent of the cast near to perfection.

After its first week-long run at the Atlanta Theatre, the play returned there in January of the following year. By 1938 however, the play had peaked. When she was asked why some of the seats in the theater were empty, Nellie Davis explained, "It's just because everyone in Atlanta has seen the play."

Coy Jones as the Striver, H. J. Furlow as Satan.

The chemistry of *Heaven Bound* had been exciting in more ways than one. In 1938 a new choir spun off from the Number One and Number Two choirs. It was the D. T. Babcock Gospel Chorus, named for the pastor at that time. The robust new chorus brought the rousing new gospel sound to songs such as "Come and Go to That Land" that were added to the play in the late 1930s.

Also in 1938, Henry Furlow, the young high school teacher who made quite a name for himself as Satan, and Florine Dyer, one of Heaven's pianists, were married in a quiet ceremony held in the pastor's study. With a marriage that seemed to be "made in Heaven," H. J. and Flo would become one of the most remarkable couples in the history of the church, pursuing their work and claiming their accomplishments as a team. But romance in Heaven did not stop with the Furlows. In 1938 the newly wed Ralph and Corinne Johnson were just joining the *Heaven Bound* choir, and the wedding of the Striver, Coy Jones, and the Mother's Girl, Janie Jones, was in the offing.

Aside from the love affairs blooming in the expanding choirs, Bethel Church was still claiming unique recognition among Atlanta's churches. In 1939 Choir Number Two accepted an invitation to render spirituals at the world premiere of *Gone with the Wind* at Atlanta's Loew's Grand theater. Clark Gable, Vivien Leigh, and other Hollywood greats were on hand to hear Big Bethel's choir, while thousands more who were denied the privilege lined the streets outside. "We sang and then sat down and watched the movie," recalled Edna Collier, an alto in Number Two.

All seemed well on the homefront. Roosevelt's social programs were putting people back to work. One of those programs, the Federal Theatre, had come right to the church's doorstep and carried *Heaven Bound* into mainstream theater. The play had become a hit in Atlanta and around Georgia and was flirting with national fame promised by exposure in national publications. But presentations of the play outside the South were stymied by the church's jealousy and silence about it. Truly the fortunes of *Heaven Bound* would have known no end had it not established its nest in the deep South and had the officers of Bethel Church not prevented other churches and theater companies from presenting it. *The Green Pastures,* by contrast, had taken the country by storm by the end of the thirties and had even spun off a successful movie.

But fame up North was not an objective for the keepers of Big Bethel's play. The church officers were content with their profitable local monopoly, and they guarded it with their silence.

The War Years

By the 1940s *Heaven Bound* was far more than a church play: it was a southern institution. But the play soon met yet another test of its stability. This time the challenge came not from legal strife or theatrical innovation but from natural attrition in the church. During the 1940s the play's founders, Nellie Davis and Lula Jones, died, and Dewitt Talmadge Babcock, whose tenure as pastor was the longest in the history of the church, moved on to another church. Also during these years the onerous church debt was retired and the number of *Heaven Bound* performances drastically reduced.

Nor did the play escape the influence of world events. Big Bethel, like the rest of the nation, was preoccupied with what Winston Churchill called that "monster of depravity"—war. Although the demand for military supplies and machinery stimulated the economy and put people back to work after the Depression, Big Bethelites knew they were witnessing a living hell. After several years of the protracted war, Babcock began to show his frustration. Each time the church presented *Heaven Bound* he threatened to suspend the singing of the old black spiritual "Ain't Gonna Study War No More" because its lyrics seemed to offer nothing but a dose of wishful thinking.

Several of Big Bethel's young men joined the half-million blacks who fought in the armed forces. Thelba Brown was just beginning to look back nostalgically on his boyhood in Big Bethel. He had enjoyed singing in the Junior Choir, where he pulled the pigtails of the girls in the group. He even took pleasure in recalling the chore he regularly performed for the church: cleaning out the belfry where the pigeons nested, far up in the church's east tower. Just a few years later, Thelba, now a grown man, landed at Normandy Beach on D-Day. There were others. The Dansby family, well established in Bethel Church, sent their young Oscar to join up. And the Greens, equally prominent in the church, said goodbye to their son Julius.

Julius Green, a sailor on the battleship *Texas,* left Big Bethel for the South Pacific theater, taking with him fond memories of the church and the play. One afternoon in 1943 Julius found time to browse through a *Life* magazine. In it he stumbled upon a pictorial essay entitled "Heaven Bound." Although Julius quickly realized the play featured in the article was not Big Bethel's *Heaven*

Bound but an imitation by a Baptist church in Richmond, Virginia, the mere name of the play stirred a wave of homesickness. After the war Julius, a lifelong member of Big Bethel, joined the production staff of *Heaven Bound* and eventually became lighting and sound supervisor.

A CHANGE OF PACE

By the time the war years arrived, *Heaven Bound* had already crystallized in the form it kept for the next fifty years. The number and character of the pilgrims and the songs they sang did not change again. Like Atlanta itself, the play had grown in stature and was as much a part of the city as Coca-Cola and *Gone with the Wind.* Students, scholars, patrons of the theater, and church groups from all over the Southeast were eager to see it. To accommodate crowds numbering in the thousands, Big Bethel was still staging the play at the Municipal Auditorium.

Heaven Bound continued to be a vital means of paying the church's tremendous debt. Although a few of the members were affluent, most held low-paying jobs as maids, cooks, butlers, and manual laborers. Casting about for ways to supplement the church's income, one member suggested that more money could be made from the play if only the church would allow a "colored night" and a "white night." That suggestion was shelved.

Although the play was a box-office hit, a serious accident curtailed the feverish pace of production around 1940. The accident occurred at a private performance sponsored by the Coca-Cola Company's Robert Woodruff at the Municipal Auditorium. While the curtain was down for intermission, a whole section of a platform built for the Angels ripped away from the underlying supports. An entire band of Angels—seventeen in all—fell out of Heaven. John Calhoun, one of the husky Guardian Angels, fell on the leg of Dorothy Flemister, the school nurse who played the Pilgrim to Zion. Flemister walked with a limp for the rest of her life. Ruby Robinson, the Mother's Girl, lost her unborn child because of the fall. Florine Furlow, who was seated at the piano, stopped playing when she saw her husband, playing Satan, disappear behind the rubble. The injured were taken first to Grady Hospital and later to Harris Hospital, an institution for blacks. Woodruff paid the medical expenses.

The officers of the church were reluctant to allow the play to be performed outside the church again. As the accident had clearly shown, hastily built stage sets in rented auditoriums could cause injuries and even fatalities. The only really safe place for the play appeared to be the Bethel sanctuary, where it was meant to be performed in the first place. The trustees of the church therefore formulated a policy restricting the play to the sanctuary. With the liquidation of the church's debt now in sight, the trustees also limited the number of performances to two nights per year, thereby retiring the play as a principal money-making tool for the church. These restrictions remained in effect for the next fifty years.

A RIDERLESS HORSE

After filing her copyright suit against both the church and Nellie Davis in 1931, Jones never again performed in the play. B. G. Dawson, who was pastor when Jones filed her suit, had banned her from the choir, and she did not seek reinstatement after he left the church. She remained bitter until she died in 1940.

Jones never understood the intricacies of copyright law, which at first allowed her the legal status of author of the play and later offered no protection against others seeking to take the honor away from her. She understood only that she had brought a valuable idea to the church and got nothing for it. She felt that the play had been taken from her because she was not a lettered person and given to Nellie Davis, who was. Davis had used her rare combination of gifts to lift Lula Jones's humble idea to a level of great prominence. Davis pulled down the lion's share of the recognition, and Jones never forgot it. To train other church choirs to perform the play, Davis traveled all over the state, expanding her reputation and presumably earning money for her efforts. Everybody profited from the play, Jones thought, except herself.

Lula Jones's bitterness must have caused Davis great discomfort. But neither the resentment the two women had for each other nor their desire for individual gain and recognition could obscure the greatness of their joint work. They gave to the masses a unique ministry of music and drama and to the world of the performing arts a theatrical masterpiece. Lula Byrd Jones's idea ensured for her a prominent place in Big Bethel's history.

Unlike Jones's death, which caused little reaction in the church, Nellie Davis's terminal illness had a stunning effect on the church, the play, and the community. Davis died in the prime of her life. She had just completed, with honors, a graduate program in English literature at the University of Cincinnati and had a promising career ahead of her as a college professor.

Davis had no children and was separated from her husband when she died. In 1918, at the age of sixteen, she had given up her membership at nearby Allen Temple A.M.E. Church to join Big Bethel. Although her only brother also joined Bethel, her parents remained at a sister church—Wheat Street—just a little farther up Auburn Avenue. Now *Heaven Bound* was turning out to be the crowning achievement in an otherwise unfinished life.

Davis had been ill for a while and had known since the fall of 1943 that she would not live long. She talked about her illness with a few choir members who had become her close friends. One of those friends was Daisy Payne Brown, the play's legendary Hypocrite. Davis broke the news to Brown one night after a choir rehearsal at the church. Sobbing in Brown's arms, Davis confided that her physician had just diagnosed her illness: leukemia.

Because of her poor health, Davis had already begun to withdraw from *Heaven Bound.* Wyolene Pullum, Davis's protege, had already been named the Atlanta director, and Henry Furlow was serving as Pullum's assistant. For a while Davis struggled on, buoyed up by each day she lived beyond the doctor's prediction. But finally, in June 1944, the end came. She was forty-two years old.

She was "widely known and prominent in religious, educational and civic circles," reported the *Atlanta Daily World,* after covering Davis's funeral. Black and white, rich and poor crowded into Bethel Church for Davis's funeral on a hot June afternoon. People in the Auburn Avenue community came to say goodbye, and Clark College, where she had taught, sent a delegation of professors, along with its college choir, to represent the school. Several preachers also brought warm words of tribute from the neighboring churches. William Holmes Borders, pastor of Wheat Street Church, said Davis "touched this community at all points with her voice, her soul and her life." Probably the most poignant tribute was a wreath from her own choir—Choir Number One. It was an unusual wreath that stood tall beside the coffin. Flowers of contrasting colors were arranged to spell out an epitaph for Nellie Beatrice Lindley Davis: HEAVEN BOUND!

Heaven Bound had never been performed without Davis at the helm. Although various choir members helped her direct and produce the play, it had always been clear that *Heaven Bound* was really Davis's show. She wrote the Scroll Reading, directed the drama, and served as chorister of the Celestial Choir. She also played key roles. To the community outside the church, Davis was the play's spokesperson and its ambassador of goodwill. Without her, *Heaven Bound* was like a riderless horse.

From her sick bed Davis had anointed Leslie Nolan as the new chorister of Choir Number One. Nolan was an intelligent, personable woman and a good chorister. She worked on the west end of Auburn Avenue at the Atlanta Life Insurance Company. In the play Nolan had been cast by Davis for the role of the Pilgrim of Sorrow. Garbed in the long black mourning veil appointed for that role, Nolan would trudge through the aisles of the church, facing down the blandishments of Satan, while singing the soulful spiritual, "Nobody Knows the Trouble I've Seen."

While Nolan stepped into Davis's shoes as chorister of Choir Number One, Wyolene Pullum carried on as the acting director of *Heaven Bound.* Pullum had held the post through the illness and death of Nellie Davis. Although both

Nolan and Pullum were honorable candidates for the directorship of *Heaven Bound,* neither brought to the post Davis's multiplicity of strengths.

The absence of a clear leader for the famous play left Pastor Babcock at one of the most significant crossroads in the church's history. One nagging problem he faced was the reluctance of Choir Number One to give up control of the play. *Heaven Bound* was their brainchild, and many of their members had watched it grow from the very beginning. During Nellie Davis's life the members of this older choir clearly dominated the play, holding practically all of the leading roles but that of Satan. Members of Number One could hardly bear the thought that someone from the younger adult choir, Number Two, might take over their play.

But this was no time for the church to be embarrassed by a *Heaven Bound* floundering for lack of a leader. The Bethel congregation, now seventy-five years beyond Emancipation, and a hundred years beyond its origin in the Union Church, was the oldest and most accomplished black congregation in Atlanta. Indeed, Bethel Church had become a leading religious and social institution in the South, and *Heaven Bound* was the jewel in its crown. This was no time to come up short.

Babcock had to make a decision. For the sake of the play, the new leader would have to reflect the attributes of Nellie Davis that had made the play great. Davis loved the church, the play, and the people. She was a creature of the arts, a person to whom music and drama were second nature. A gifted leader, she knew how to organize people and prod them toward excellence. Babcock wisely chose the only person in the church who approached Davis's stature: the charismatic Henry James Furlow, Satan.

THE RISE OF THE FURLOWS

Although Leslie Nolan did not resist Furlow's appointment as director of *Heaven Bound,* it stirred long-lasting resentment among the other members of Number One. Indeed, for some of Number One's members, handing over *Heaven Bound* to the young chorister of Number Two was almost too much to bear. They had hoped for a director from their own ranks. Still loyal to Nellie Davis, they felt that Furlow and his choir had hijacked their play.

Both Henry Furlow and his wife, Florine, grew up in Bethel Church and had roots there reaching back toward Reconstruction. Both of them also came up through the ranks of Choir Number Two. Although not among the original cast, Florine Furlow joined *Heaven Bound* during its first year, when Number Two was invited to help Number One meet the increasing demand for performances. Henry Furlow joined the play's Celestial Choir three years later.

Like Nellie Davis, Henry Furlow was a graduate of Atlanta University and was visibly excited about the learning he had acquired there. Also like Davis, Furlow was a gifted singer and had carved out a place for himself as a star in the play. Adding to his clout as director of *Heaven Bound* was another new appointment: he was named chorister of Choir Number Two to replace Helen ("Ma") Massey after her death in the late 1940s.

Unlike Nellie Davis, however, Furlow did not work alone. His accomplishments at Bethel Church almost always emerged from teamwork with his wife. Although Furlow could flap his wings like a falcon and snatch his head like Toscanini, he could not read a note of music; Florine could read music and had played keyboard instruments since early childhood. A consummate musician, Florine played for her husband's choir and accompanied his tenor solos. She brought to the play not only talent but character and high ideals as well.

Emmie Florine Dyer was born on Auburn Avenue, just up the street from Big Bethel, and her roots ran deep into the history of the church. Motherless at the age of four, she was mentored by her father, a former slave. From the hills of Tennessee, Caleb Dyer had brought his family to Atlanta's Old Bethel in 1882. Coming of age when blacks were still learning the responsibilities of freedom, his youngest daughter, Florine, was impassioned with virtues that would lift the proverbial veil of ignorance from her people. In addition to her schoolteacher ideals and her fine musicianship, she built love into the play—fifty-six years of it. And with the powerful tool of quiet consistency—the tool of the master teacher—she tuned the voices, corrected the grammar, and cleared the diction of scores of players.

She was also good with people. In her self-effacing manner, she shared with her husband keen insights about human nature that helped him deal with the various personalities in the choirs. Dark and impeccably poised, Florine Furlow was a thoroughly cultured woman. With advanced degrees from Columbia and Atlanta universities, she was also a fine educator. Her strong, gentle presence not only complemented her husband's authority but served notice that she was a force in her own right.

Known for his formality and a distinctive, foot-dragging gait, Henry Furlow was a dramatic man on stage and off. His hair had turned white long before its time, and it contrasted with his dark complexion to give him a distinguished look. Some felt that Furlow's conspicuously proper enunciation was haughty, if not downright arrogant. Others regarded it simply as a carry-over of Satan's affectations in the play.

Watching Furlow take charge in rehearsal was no ordinary experience. Facing the players, who were seated in the pews, he positioned himself in the center front of the church, where bodies lay in state. In that spot, which came to symbolize his authority and status in the play, he would crisscross his arms around his shoulders, fix his eyes on the ceiling, and lean back slightly on the altar behind him. Silence fell over the cast, and Furlow, from that point on, was the unquestioned boss.

Once rehearsals began, an unstated rule permitted only positive thoughts about *Heaven Bound.* If the Furlows did not make that rule, they certainly abided by it and sometimes vigorously enforced it. "Talk it up!" Furlow used to say in rehearsal, urging everyone to spread the word of the coming performance.

The Furlows directed *Heaven Bound* with the courtly grace and manners that were typical of their generation and social class. During rehearsal they addressed each other, sometimes even in extended conversation, with the utmost formality. "Mr. Furlow, it's time to start the rehearsal," Florine would say to Henry, pointing to her watch. "Yes, Mrs. Furlow, we're going to start right now," he would answer. Only their closest friends heard them address each other more intimately, as "Dick" and "Flo." Not only did the Furlows perform and direct *Heaven Bound,* like the old-fashioned classroom teachers that they were, they also taught it. They made the sanctuary their classroom and the players their students. Furlow's Satan was a hit with *Heaven Bound* audiences. He pranced and capered about the auditorium with unusual agility and balance, wearing his horns at a roguish angle. Drawing a small bouquet, an apple, or a parasol from beneath his cape, he distracted the vulnerable Pilgrims from the prize toward which they were stumbling. An accomplished acrobat Furlow liked to show off his talent in stunning theatrical feats. He sometimes stood on his head and pointed his feet straight up above him. While his viewers shrieked in amazement, he would leap from the case of the grand piano, his flaming red cape fluttering in midair. At the finale Furlow would take off his horns and position himself in the very center of the white-robed angels. There, with his marvelous tenor voice, he would sing the old black spiritual for which many in the audience waited from one year to the next, "Hand Me Down the Silver Trumpet, Gabriel."

Furlow loved the play, but he also made good practical use of it. He had a way of increasing his own personal stock with the powerful whites who came to see *Heaven Bound.* He knew their preferences, their tastes, and their sensitivities. He also knew they expected not only spiritual fulfillment from the play but theatrical entertainment from him. In appreciation of the show Furlow always put on for them, the whites sent him stacks of fan mail after the close of each season.

Furlow's methods were not unlike the old "shrewd acquiescence" used by many African Americans of his generation to get favors from the powerful whites. Ira Jarrell, the superintendent of the Atlanta public schools, was one

Henry Furlow, as Satan, atop the grand piano. Florine Furlow is at the keyboard.

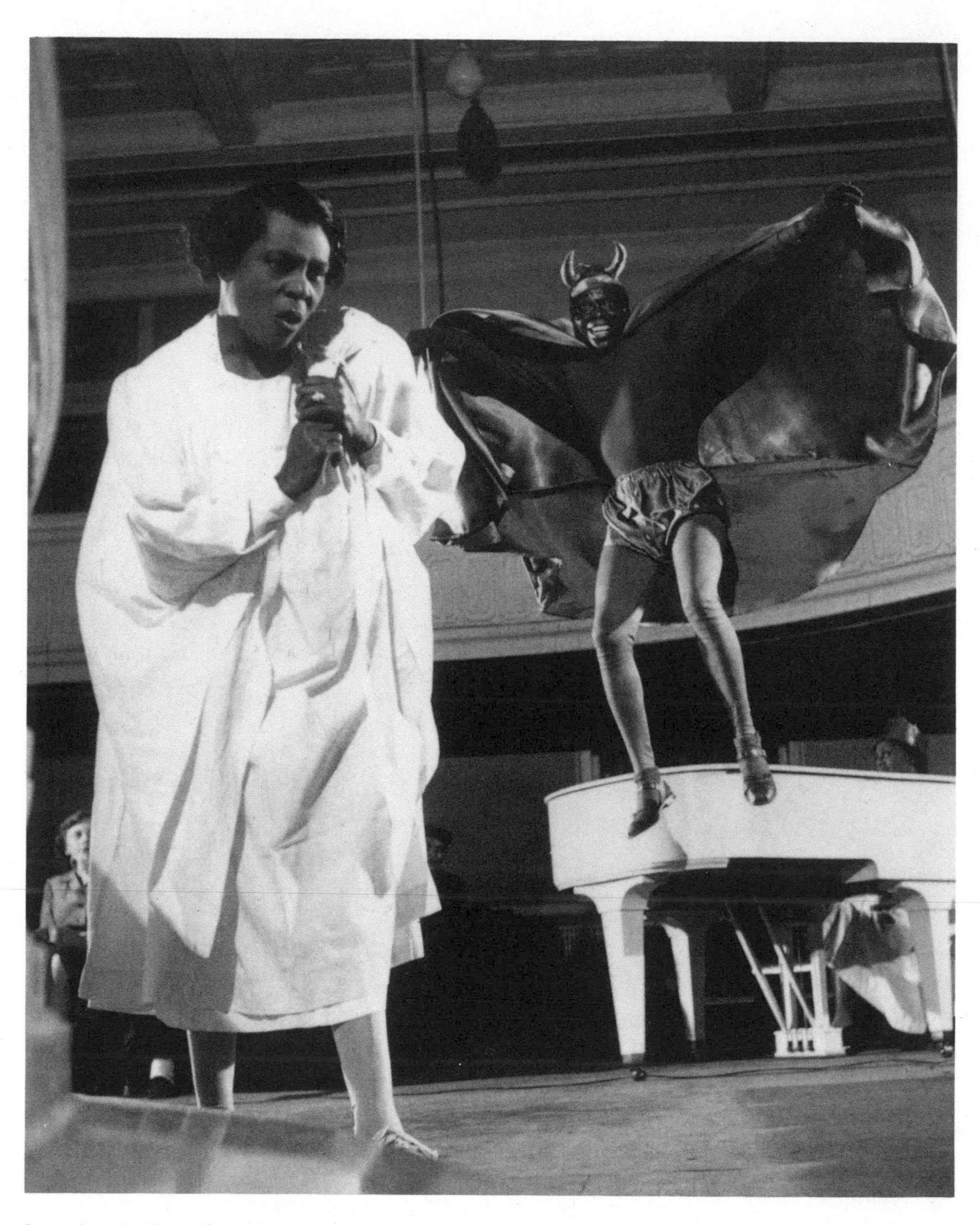

Satan leaping from the piano.

Satan stalks the Pilgrim of the Cross, Huellen Morgan.

of the influential whites regularly in Furlow's audiences. Furlow and his wife both taught in the public schools, and Jarrell was their boss. At *Heaven Bound* performances, Furlow roped off seats in the front of the church for Jarrell and the rest of the members of the Atlanta Board of Education.

The notoriety of the play and the special place of the Furlows in it could not escape Jarrell's notice. The newspapers raved about *Heaven Bound,* noting its unique role in improving interracial relations and enriching religious life in Atlanta. Prominent Atlantans praised the Furlows' work. Although both the Furlows were known to be excellent teachers, Jarrell's fondness for their church work undoubtedly boosted their careers. Florine was named principal of a school in 1946, and Henry Furlow was offered but declined a similar promotion.

Although he was a stunning success with *Heaven Bound* audiences, Furlow could not claim quick popularity with the members of Choir Number One. Some of his decisions did not help matters. As the new director, he quickly gave more key roles in the play to members of his own choir. Huellen Morgan, for example, took the role of the Pilgrim of the Cross, and Susie Chapman took the role of the Burden-Bearer. Furlow also retired Ruby Lloyd—an original cast member—from the role of the Scroll Reader and replaced her with Emellen Estes, a younger member of Choir Number One.

Furlow's appointment of his wife as the organist for *Heaven Bound* was another sore point with the members of Number One. Although Florine had always played Big Bethel's piano, Clara Edwards, a music teacher and member of Number One, had been the official church organist for all the choirs and the undisputed organist for *Heaven Bound.* When Edwards died, her daughter, Maurece, succeeded her for a short while. Soon afterward, however, Maurece abruptly left the organ and departed from the church, never to return. Two explanations for Maurece's exit circulated among church members. According to one, Pastor Babcock overrode the preference of Choir Number One to have Maurece as its organist and instead selected Harriette Enous, a talented young keyboardist from Number Two. The other explanation pointed the finger at Henry Furlow as the person responsible for Maurece's departure. In a rehearsal for *Heaven Bound,* Furlow reportedly asked Florine to leave the piano and "take the organ." Maurece, already seated at the organ, refused to move and said to Furlow, "I'm taking my mother's place." When Furlow insisted, Maurece reportedly left the church and never came back.

Although Furlow was controversial, most people—especially his students and *Heaven Bound* fans—found him a likable fellow. Beyond the question of his popularity, however, Furlow thoroughly understood the mission of *Heaven Bound* and his role in it. He understood that Satan was not just an entertainer but an actual force of evil in the lives of the play's viewers. Matchless in his portrayal of Satan, Furlow heightened the tension between good and evil in

Satan sitting in the audience.

Saint Peter and the Pilgrim to Zion, Dora Morgan, on her way to Heaven.

the play and made vividly clear the consequences of making the wrong choice. Years later, in a 1978 television interview, he explained his role: "It's my job to take them to hell, every one of them. And I am making that effort as realistically as I possibly can."

THE DEBT IS PAID

Pastor Babcock had seen *Heaven Bound* through it all. The play was only four years old when he came to the church in 1934. Through the Depression and a war, he watched it flourish. He fostered an atmosphere in which the warring factions of Nellie Davis and Lula Jones could coexist with civility and tolerance. He preached the funerals of both the play's founders and appointed a man that history would confirm as the right choice to lead the play through the next four decades.

In 1945 Babcock, with the help of thousands of dollars brought in by the play, proved the truth of his motto, "It Can Be Done." Under his leadership the congregation paid off the enormous debt that had originally propelled the *Heaven Bound* idea. None but the pastor and members who struggled with it could have known the strain of the debt. At one point Babcock had been driven to appeal to Governor Eugene Talmadge for help in avoiding a foreclosure on the mortgage. Babcock's shrewdness and perseverance paid off. The mortgage was burned, and a plaque was affixed to the church in celebration of the achievement.

In 1948 Babcock was assigned to another church, in Savannah. Even though the Methodist system of rotating pastoral ministry was supposed to be good for the church and good for the pastor, it was hard for Big Bethelites to think about getting along without Babcock. His strengths were formidable. In another era he might have played a larger role in social activism, but in the 1930s and 1940s both he and the church were preoccupied with the war, the Depression, and liquidation of the debt. In spite of these difficulties, his fourteen-year ministry was fruitful for Big Bethel and the most fruitful ever for the play. Though pastors would come and go, the church would not soon forget his extraordinary achievements.

The Winds of Change

Its course well charted by Dewitt Babcock, *Heaven Bound* reached the 1950s well intact. The diversity of the play's audiences reflected its popularity in every sector of the community. With the church's debt paid off, however, the production schedule continued at the more relaxed pace it adopted at the start of the 1940s.

But the times were very different. In 1938, when *Heaven Bound* returned by popular demand for a second run at the Atlanta Theatre, Nellie Davis had boasted that it was hard to find Atlantans who had not seen the play. Davis's claim, although probably overstated, underscored the tremendous popularity of the play in the early days. During the 1950s, however, the once-stable world in which *Heaven Bound* had existed was fundamentally changing.

By 1950 a new Atlanta had arisen from the ruins of a city devastated by the Union Army almost a hundred years before. The city was a thriving metropolis, poised for dramatic growth. A regional railroad center, it was strategically located to become the hub of trade, transportation, and commerce in the Southeast.

As Atlanta grew during the 1950s, vast numbers of inner-city residents—including a large portion of Big Bethel's congregation—began moving out to the ever-expanding suburbs. The slowdown in the growth of the downtown congregation created problems in the aging cast. Finding good, strong replacements who would stick with the play and love it became a challenge. The congregation, moreover, was becoming more educated, more affluent, and also more worldly-wise and blasé. It remained to be seen whether the play could hold on to the passion and power that had fired the religion and imagination of the first generation of players.

Heaven Bound, with its committed old players, charted a new future in the changing environment. This it did while retaining its magical lure and a message that was simple, powerful, and timeless: good ultimately triumphs over evil.

THE NEW PASTOR—A BOON TO THE PLAY

After the Babcock years and the brief pastorate of D. V. Kyle, the church received a new pastor in 1951. Harold Irvin Bearden wasted no time building on the church's record of achievements. His fiery but practical sermons were broadcast throughout Atlanta by the city's first black-owned radio station, WERD—a "first" among black parish ministries. Quickly Bearden made the church's pulpit part of the vanguard of the civil rights movement, which was taking shape right on Auburn Avenue. He was also a shrewd political maneuverer whose love for all types of people made him a very popular pastor, and one day a bishop.

Bearden proved himself a great friend to the play. He had keen sensibilities and a bent for historical accuracy. Showing great interest in *Heaven Bound,* he investigated its origin in an attempt once again to ration the credit properly between Nellie Davis and Lula Jones. Thelma Jones Belt, the stepdaughter of Lula Jones and a lifelong member of Bethel Church, remembered Bearden's concern. What bothered him was the possibility that others had refused to recognize Lula Jones as the author of the play simply because she worked in a laundry and lacked extensive formal training. Belt and her brother, Henry Jones Jr., harbored the same suspicion.

Bearden phoned Belt one Sunday morning, urging her to attend the Sunday morning worship service. He promised to set the record straight, once and for all, that morning. To Belt's delight, Bearden made good on his promise. He chided the congregation about its elitist tendencies and portrayed Lula Jones as worthy of greater respect. Her picture was eventually hung in the downstairs assembly hall of the church.

Recognizing the play as a treasure of black song and black folk culture, Bearden wanted to preserve and perpetuate *Heaven Bound.* When the *Heaven Bound* season of the year rolled around, he prepared the church people for its presentation and allowed nothing to get in the way. He even concluded the Sunday worship services by asking everybody to look up to the ceiling and say "Heaven bound" and then look at each other and say the same. To Bearden, the play was supreme in the life and history of Bethel Church.

NATIONAL EXPOSURE IN *LIFE* MAGAZINE

During the first thirty years of the play, Atlanta's population expanded from 360,000 to one million. With this growth came a greater variety of theater groups and cultural events that competed with each other. Adding to the competition was a new technological phenomenon, the television, which was

Above: The full congregation on a Sunday morning. *Below:* Leroy Russell plays the Preacher in Heaven.

beaming all sorts of entertainment into an increasing number of living rooms. It appeared that *Heaven Bound* might be lost in the shuffle. Many of the city's newer residents probably had never heard about *Heaven Bound.* Others were more interested in television or other attractions around the city. It was a new day, and *Heaven Bound* could no longer rest on its laurels as the premier black cultural event in Atlanta. It had to find new ways to compete.

At this critical time in its history, the play got some breaks. In January 1953, more than a decade after *Heaven Bound* had last made headlines, *Life* magazine featured a complete pictorial essay that renewed the prestige of Big Bethel's play. One of the photographs, the picture of Furlow grinning diabolically in his Satanic horns, became a trademark by which people from coast to coast came to know the play. The essay made it clear that *Heaven Bound* was still working the old magic with which it had charmed audiences back in the 1930s.

Another bit of good fortune that befell the play was the newspaper coverage started by Celestine Sibley, a young columnist with the *Atlanta Constitution.* Prodded by the newspaper's publisher, Ralph McGill, Sibley saw the play for the first time one autumn night in 1953. She was entranced: "If there's anybody in Atlanta besides me who waited 23 years to see the Big Bethel A.M.E. Church's presentation of 'Heaven Bound,' they don't know what they're missing. . . . It's the best thing I ever saw, here or in Hollywood." So impressed was Sibley with the play that she wrote a column about it almost every year thereafter.

SWEET AUBURN—AN EXTENSION OF THE CHURCH AND THE PLAY

Auburn Avenue was a fitting home for *Heaven Bound.* From its rise in the late 1890s to its decline in the 1960s, this thoroughfare, with its tributaries from all over Atlanta's predominantly black Fourth Ward, nourished a complete subculture where the black pilgrimage in America reached some of its highest plateaus. But while the play was enjoying nationwide publicity, Auburn Avenue, its home base, was approaching a point of decline.

To Bethel Church, Auburn Avenue was not simply an isolated world outside the walls of the church. The church's pastors went out onto the street and ministered to the drunks and derelicts in the billiard rooms and on the corners. The church's members found employment in Auburn Avenue businesses. Women raising money for the church strolled this black "Main Street," selling fried-chicken, fish, and soul-food dinners to the barbers and beauticians, the lawyers and physicians. And, though they kept it quiet, many of the church's members went out at night to enjoy entertainment in the clubs on Auburn Avenue. Indeed, black church life and black secular life formed a continuum: it was difficult to know where one stopped and the other began. According to

The Wayward Girl, played by Bernice Gross.

The Wayward Girl, denied admittance at the Pearly Gates.

Auburn Avenue. Big Bethel's steeple is visible in the distance.

James Cone, a prominent A.M.E. theologian, the black Christian faith search out meaning "in the spirituals and the blues, folklore and sermon . . . in the rhythm, the beat and the swing of life . . . whether on Saturday night or Sunday morning." Auburn Avenue was as much a part of Bethel Church as the preacher and the choir.

Dubbed "Sweet Auburn" back in the 1930s because of the cash that flowed through successful black businesses, the thoroughfare was still the hub of black existence in the 1950s. The front steps of the church afforded a panoramic view of life on Sweet Auburn. On sweltering Saturday afternoons during the summer months, the Eastern Stars and the Elks turned out in large parades. Garbed in plumed hats, white gloves, and ceremonial aprons, members of these secret societies were joined by bands from local black schools, military units, and tagalongs from the neighborhood.

On weekdays, the lobbies of black-owned banks and insurance companies and the offices of black lawyers, physicians, and dentists and pharmacies filled

The Striver, Coy Jones, sweeps through the Pearly Gates, his eye still on Satan.

with black customers, clients, and patients. Lively talk, on subjects ranging from the gravest issues to the lowest scuttlebutt, was aired in the crowded barber shops and beauty parlors. The merchants met for lunch at soul-food places like Henry's Grill, Hawks' Dinette, Beamon's, or Yates Drugs. Big Bethel's parsonage was on the eastern end of Auburn Avenue, closer to the Baptist sister churches, Ebenezer and Wheat Street. Up there the aroma of fried chicken from Edwards soul-food restaurant permeated the air. In the evenings, Auburn Avenue nightclubs such as the Silver Streak and the Peacock came alive with neon lights and entertainment by local talent. Occasionally such luminaries as Dinah Washington, Nat King Cole, and Little Richard performed in the nightclubs.

Heaven Bound was part of this larger Auburn Avenue culture. Not only did the play reflect the religious life of Big Bethel and the high level of literacy that had brought successful commerce to the community, it also mirrored the total spectrum of life along this national black oasis. The frivolous Wayward Girl, the Gamblers, the Striver, and the Pilgrim of Faith were not simply characters in a play. They were replicas of real people out on Auburn Avenue, people who preached and prophesied on the street corners, people who sang and danced in the clubs and juke joints, people who joked and told tales in the rib shacks and parlors. Some of the Auburn Avenue characters worshiped in the churches and fraternized in the secret societies. Others gambled on the corners. For the *Heaven Bound* players, the mores and folkways of Auburn Avenue were the best possible lessons in drama. Sometimes the people having fun on the avenue were the players themselves.

Although life in the 1950s and 1960s seemed to hum along pleasantly on Auburn Avenue, for black Atlantans urban relocation and the great thrust toward integration were shifting the center of gravity away from this restricted world. They now looked toward the approaching reality of access to the downtown restaurants, hotels, shops, and theaters, where the walls of segregation soon fell.

The approaching decline of Auburn Avenue as the cultural, social, and economic base of black Atlanta raised questions about the future of *Heaven Bound.* It appeared the play would be left without a support system. Years later, the congregation found itself struggling to recover the ambiance of culture and progress that once nurtured the play and its players.

SUCCESSION IN THE PLAY

At the end of the 1950s, only eight of the original thirty-four players were still living, with seven of them still performing in the play. As the growth of the congregation slowed and the underpinnings of Auburn Avenue culture began

The Christian, Renita Phillips, implores the Gamblers, Harold Murray and John Bolton.

to give way, the stable old members of the congregation—those who had followed in the footsteps of the very first *Heaven Bound* players—were heavily relied upon to keep the play going. Indeed, these members were the lifeline between the play and future generations of Big Bethel.

Dorothy Buggs Flemister was a fine example of the loyalty, if not stubbornness, with which older Big Bethelites carried forward the play. Flemister, a school nurse by profession, was one of the angels who had fallen out of Heaven when the stage set had collapsed at the Municipal Auditorium. She had also played the Pilgrim to Zion and the Determined Soul. Like Satan, the Soldier, and other long-term players, Flemister became a fixture in the play. After a long *Heaven Bound* career, she approached the end of life feeling that her role should be passed down within the family of seasoned players. On her deathbed, she summoned Evvie Smith Mabry, another longtime member of the cast, and asked Mabry to take her role, the Determined Soul. Mabry agreed. Requests like Flemister's were not uncommon among the older players; indeed, legacies seemed to have become the normal way of transferring roles.

Faithful members like Flemister had kept the church a safe place for *Heaven Bound.* They had sustained the play, year after year, by oral tradition and by the slow process of inbreeding that had yielded perfection over the years. Demographic shifts in the community, however, were threatening this method of preserving the play. The population of the church was beginning to decline, and a quicker way had to be found to train a new generation of players.

Luckily, the old-timers were not so stubborn about their roles and their inbreeding technique that they did not see the danger of having too few replacements. Not only was there no time to wait for another generation to grow up in the play, but the number of people growing up in the church was getting smaller. Beginning in the 1950s, the old players found themselves relaxing the standards a bit and training some altogether new people.

This next generation of *Heaven Bound* players included several absolutely outstanding young performers. One of the talented neophytes was Anita Brown Glover, a coloratura soprano with few peers in the region. With her gifted, trained voice, Glover took the role of the Mother's Girl—a character struggling mightily against Satan's temptations in the hope of reuniting with her mother in Heaven. On performance night Anita, along with the other Pilgrims awaiting their turns to perform, sat on a pew in the back of the darkened church. Rising to meet the spotlight, she smiled confidently before plunging the audience into a deep sadness with the song of the motherless child—"Tell Mother I'll Be There." Slowly down the aisle she came, weaving around Satan and his traps, making her way toward Heaven. On reaching the center of the altar, she fell to her knees and gazed upward at her mother, who was beckoning from Heaven with outstretched arms. While Anita bowed her head in prayer,

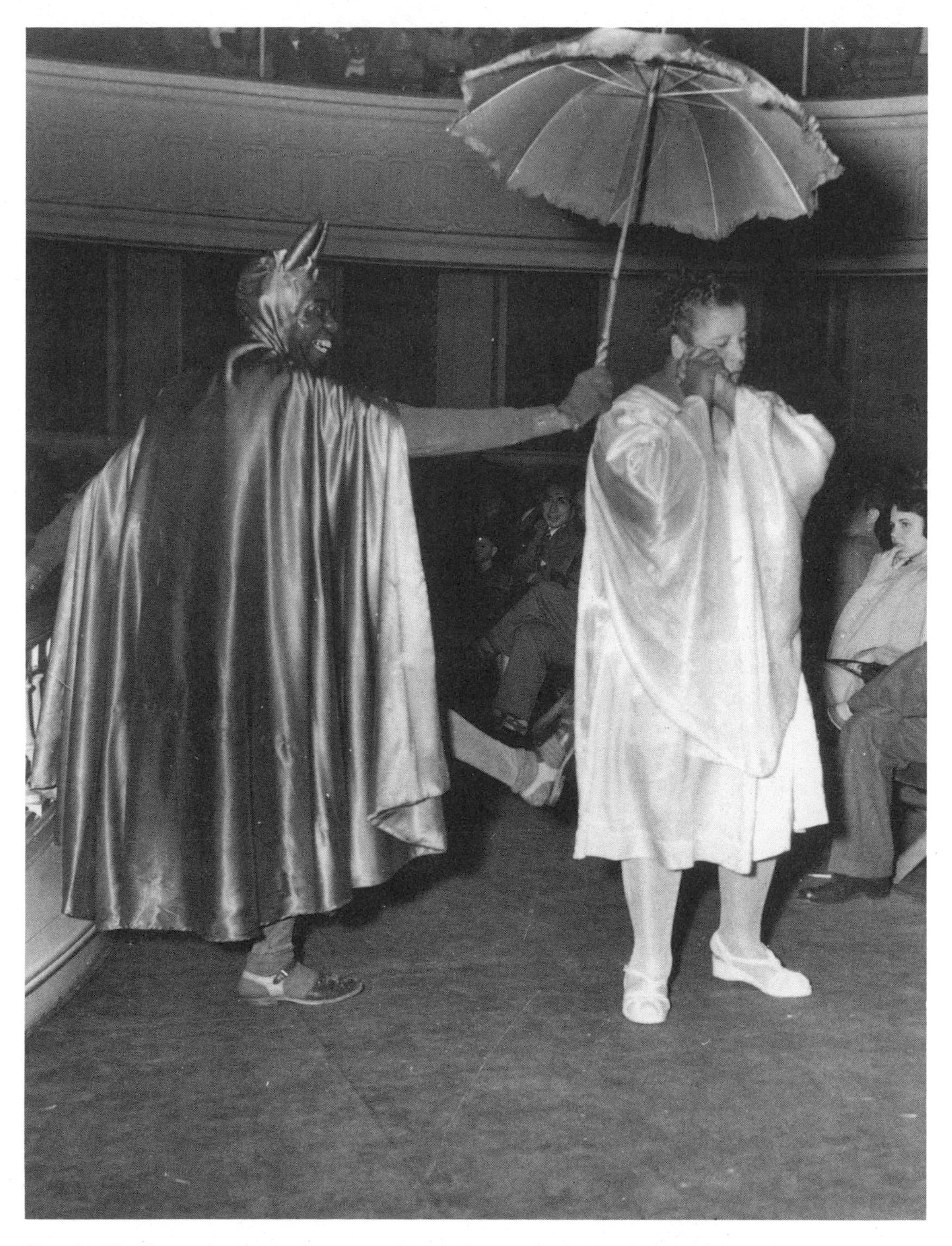

Dorothy Flemister, playing the Determined Soul. Near the end of her life, Flemister "bequeathed" her role to another long-time player.

Satan, repelled by her praying, prowled in the background. In a split second filled with suspense, she rose and ran with lightning speed toward the Pearly Gates. The astonished audience thundered with applause as the Mother's Girl, tailed closely by Satan, swept through the Gates, into the arms of her rejoicing mother.

Anita's role, like many in the play, touched the other players as deeply as it touched the audience. One player who always seemed moved by it was Ebenezer Wood, the associate pastor of the church, who was working himself into the role of the Pilgrim of Faith. Wood, a descendant of the first free black pastor of the congregation, Joseph Wood, was also a motherless child. He buried his tearful face in his hands while Anita sang, and it was always a struggle for him to regain his composure in time to begin his performance. But when the Scroll Reader announced the appearance of the Pilgrim of Faith, Wood slowly rose from the rear pew and found his way into the spotlight. Pacing himself briskly down the aisle, he sang the spiritual "Don't Let Nobody Turn You Round!" As he moved, his voice cleared itself of its deep sadness and steadily gained strength.

Morris Gillon, a magnificent bass who played the Reformed Drunkard, was another second-generation player who became a favorite. When Gillon performed, the packed church was silent as a tomb. In a lifelike portrayal of withdrawal Gillon looked first at his bottle of liquor and then up into Heaven. Meanwhile, the peripatetic Satan cavorted with the audience and laughed at his predicament from afar. Suddenly an Angel from Heaven threw out a lifeline to rescue Gillon from hopeless deadlock. Gillon caught and held on to the lifeline while the Angel reeled him in to the Promised Land. Caught off guard by the sudden rescue, Satan ran hopelessly after his Heaven-bound prey.

Ralph Johnson, the Striver, worked as a waiter at Atlanta's exclusive, white-only Capital City Club. Since 1938 he had sung in the choir and taken part in the play. It was Johnson who pointed out for the rising young players the all-important ingredient for an effective performance. "*Heaven Bound* is something you have to feel!" he would say to them. Henry Furlow and several older players often looked for this inner feeling when choosing and coaching young replacements. They knew that sensitivity to the hardships of real life had to be reflected in the characters of the play. The young players seemed to understand. One of the new men who played the Reformed Drunkard, for example, was a recovering alcoholic in real life. In performances that mesmerized audiences, he dramatized the painful temptation, the gripping tremens he had experienced. The real-life limp of Frances Glenn, the new Bedridden Soul, lent credibility to her acting. More than any dramatic coaching, it was the experience of life's predicaments—illness, loneliness, addiction, problems on the job, in marriage, or at school—that made the players consummate actors who rendered stunning performances.

Satan tempts the Mother's Girl, Janie Jones, who looks beyond temptation to the promised land.

Ebenezer Wood, a second-generation player and descendant of the first black pastor of Bethel. As the Pilgrim of Faith he resists a last-minute ploy by Satan to lure him from the Pearly Gates.

The Reformed Drunkard, played by Morris Gillon, prays for strength to resist tempation.

AFFLUENCE: A MIXED BLESSING

The need to groom a new generation of players was not the only challenge facing the play in the 1950s and 1960s. Educational advancement and the increasing affluence of the congregation proved to be another. It was a curious contradiction.

In the original cast of *Heaven Bound* it was the particular combination of Big Bethel's "haves" and "have-nots" that made the play jell and gave it special, wide appeal. Educated people like Nellie Davis, Clara Edwards, and the Furlows gave the play form, elegance, and dignity. But most of the first players, like most of the parishioners during the 1930s, were unpretentious people without a great deal of formal training. Because they lived closer to questions of survival, these men and women influenced the play as no others could. Among the outstanding actors in the play were W. C. Clark, a Pullman porter, and Sarah Williams, a soprano who worked as a maid. Also a hit was the gifted contralto Esther Jordan, who eked out a living as a laundress. They gave the play color, soul, and deep religious feeling.

At the early performances of *Heaven Bound,* both the players and the black audience members "shouted" freely and openly. One viewer, writing for *Theatre Guild* magazine, captured the raw spiritual fervor of a performance in Savannah in 1931: "The sisters stir in their seats and shout 'Amen,' 'Bless de Lawd,' 'Bless you, sister!' Tears flow freely. The believers roll and quiver. . . . An old sister, weighing more than two hundred pounds, has felt the spirit but decorum must be preserved. Church officers rush to her. She protests and struggles. 'Lemme shout. I'm gonna shout anyways.' "

When the 1950s arrived, much of the spontaneity of the early church was gone. Big Bethel had become a thoroughly middle-class congregation. The "shout"—the response that marked the highest level of worship, when the Holy Spirit entered the body, and that sometimes shook the floors and walls—was not nearly as enthusiastic as it had once been.

The attainment of education and prosperity by so many Big Bethelites was, in a sense, the answer to the prayers of the church's forefathers. More members were graduating from college—often from Morris Brown College, founded in Big Bethel Church. Many of the graduates became teachers in the public schools and, unlike their parents and grandparents, were beginning to achieve financial security. Women in designer hats and men in expensive suits flaunted their prosperity in church on Sunday mornings. They traveled more, and many members owned comfortable cars, which they parked in the garages of their spacious suburban houses.

As more and more members of Big Bethel attained middle-class status, they also adopted a middle-class code of social conduct. This new code—meticu-

Effie O'Neal Porter, the Pilgrim to the Promised Land, shouts at Heaven's gate.

Parishioners Sallie Braswell (left) and Kizzie Daniel outside the church after Sunday morning worship.

lous propriety in dress, in dining, in bearing, and in speech—also extended to worship behavior. The result was a definite toning down of emotional expression in worship services as well as in performances of the play: middle-class parishioners preferred worship services that were "ritualistic and deliberative," as in the Congregational, Presbyterian, and Episcopalian churches.

The social mores of this new class, which James Weldon Johnson had already described as "second generation respectability," raised soul-searching questions about what constituted "good religion." Was the faith of the oppressed ancestors being muzzled by those who were now socially refined and claiming a little bit of their Heaven on earth? By mimicking white middle-class behavior, as some charged, were the newly prosperous parishioners changing the essential character of the African American religious experience?

During the 1950s, restrained demeanor in worship services was not too quickly condemned inside Bethel Church. After all, such behavior had been brought into black churches from the church-founded, church-supported, and sometimes church-operated black colleges, six of which were concentrated in Atlanta. Besides offering to large numbers of blacks that coveted key to the future, education, the colleges were also giving their students a code of etiquette to go with that education. In instilling "proper" modes of behavior and expression, the black colleges, before the 1960s, looked to the cultural traditions of Europe. The spread of the newly learned European patterns of behavior into the black communities and churches was, for older black educators, precisely the result desired.

For Big Bethel Church, the educational advancement of the race had been an almost sacred vision since the time of the original congregation. Parents, grandparents, teachers, and pastors had all preached education to successive generations of young Bethelites. It was no accident that Bethel housed the first school for Atlanta's freed black children and later was the birthplace of a liberal arts college. The congregation had also produced a steady and lengthening line of educators, businessmen, and civic leaders. Because education meant progress and prestige, even parishioners who did not have very much of it mimicked the manners of those who did. After all, who could say that restrained, unemotional worshipers did not have "good religion"—good enough to get to Heaven.

While new modes of demeanor were toning down the worship services, *Heaven Bound* was allowing Big Bethel's increasingly well educated players to put their sophistication on exhibit, especially for the whites who studied them closely at each performance. Affirming their dignity, as it were, the amateur players wore their makeup and costumes like professionals and enunciated the lyrics of the songs with crisp clarity. The singing of the choir not only reflected the advanced training of Big Bethel's musicians but often showed the musical refinement of a college choir. After the performances the players chatted easily and confidently with the members of the audience. They wore their polished manners like precious, hard-earned badges of legitimacy.

Despite widespread acceptance of restrained worship behavior in Bethel Church, doubts still lingered. For some of the parishioners, educational advancement and the social mores that came with it were no substitute for free spiritual expression. Fading away from the worship tradition were the shout, the distinctly African heritage of call-and-response, and the spontaneous singing and "lining" of songs preferred in the old days by passionate worshippers like Lydia Butler and Mother Green Holmes.

These questions of class, religion, and the Big Bethel congregation would arise again thirty years later. In the meantime, fears that the play would become a purely cultural event proved unfounded. Although middle-class behavior reduced the shouts to a few amens, and the loud cries to soft tears, the play continued to move with a spiritual power that broke through social constraints. People continued to be rejuvenated, renewed, and even converted at performances of the play. This power was proof enough that *Heaven Bound* was still a religious experience.

Memories in the Making

You can see the Devil, in red satin, tempting Heaven Bound Pilgrims . . . if you're in Atlanta during the two nights the Big Bethel A.M.E. Church . . . gives its annual performances of "Heaven Bound."—*The Plymouth Traveler*

The 1960s were a perilous time. Assassinations, the Vietnam War, marijuana, hippies, and urban riots—the nation seemed to search for its very soul. For those who took part in it, the warm Christian fellowship of *Heaven Bound*—laughter, camaraderie, and sweet memories—was a welcome escape from the turmoil of the times. The common church folk who made up the cast and production staff of the play were people of humor, character, and considerable dramatic talent. They offered the kind of stability and diversion that made the church a safe place to be, and the play, a fun thing to do.

REHEARSALS

Although most of the players saw each other regularly on Sunday mornings, an amazing spirit of reunion always pervaded the first rehearsal of the season. The cast members, young and old alike, filed into the sanctuary with all the joy and banter of old acquaintances reuniting after an entire year. The spirit of common endeavor was a great unifying force in this small circle of church people and set the cast apart from the large congregation.

At the first rehearsal, Furlow instructed everybody to come to the front center of the church where the group settled down in a quiet, solemn mood. It was time for devotions—those few moments of prayer and song that were as much a part of the play as was auditioning for a part. With a sternness that was second nature to an old-fashioned classroom teacher, Furlow demanded complete silence while the pianists, Florine Furlow and Harriette Enous, played the familiar rehearsal hymn, "Down at the Cross." It was a fervent moment that removed all doubt that rehearsals, like the performances, were a religious experience.

After prayer Furlow said something about the destruction of the whole world and all the Bibles in it. The old-timers knew that it was the cue to rise and recite Bible verses. Furlow ended devotions by reciting his own favorite Bible verse, "Silver and gold have I none, but such as I have give I thee," from the Book of Acts of the Apostles. Then the rehearsal began in earnest.

Furlow assigned the solos and called the Celestial Choir to order. The business of assigning the songs was not very controversial, because most participants knew in advance that few changes would be made. The old-timers simply did not give up their roles. Several of them had performed continuously in the play since the 1930s, and others had endured long years and numerous funerals before finally getting solo parts. The mere suggestion of reassigning the roles made sparks fly. Nevertheless, the death or illness of a Pilgrim occasionally created a vacancy for which newcomers could apply. A grueling process of initiation then began. The old-timers scrutinized and criticized the newcomers, as they did anybody aspiring to come into the play. And Furlow, who led the pack, would bellow, "Don't put any curves in the music!" "Don't sit on the sacred altar!" "Sound out the *t*s and *d*s at the end of the words!" When anyone on the set attempted to assist him, Furlow snapped, "Let me run it!" As if this were not enough, the newcomers had to endure further drilling and individual grooming at Florine Furlow's piano in the basement of her home.

For those newcomers not tutored by Florine, learning the lyrics to the *Heaven Bound* music was an almost insurmountable task. Song sheets were always unforgivably scarce at the rehearsals, and on those few occasions when a song sheet was available, it was quickly snatched up at the end of the rehearsal—none for taking home! Through several performance seasons, newcomers endured the most awful misery. Standing for the two-hour performances before large audiences, they perspired nervously and smiled as though nothing were awry. Those two hours, when a sea of faces gazed curiously at their lips, must have seemed like an eternity, for the newcomers, who moved their lips vigorously, uttered not a single sound. They did not know the music. It seems that this struggle to learn the music was another one of those rites of passage created to weed out those who could not endure the training or to increase the courage of those who did. The barriers erected around the *Heaven Bound* music also made it more difficult for other churches to duplicate the play.

Sometimes rehearsals were funny, unbearably funny. A few of the people who came to audition before the cast were convinced they had a talent that simply did not exist. Such a hopeful character was a woman who came to rehearsal one night confident of getting the role for which she would audition.

Furlow drew close to her and inclined his ear to her lips as she sang. As he listened intently, his eyes widened and his expression grew strained, pained. He then stopped the instruments and asked the auditioner to sing a cappella. The poor woman let out a strong yodel, Furlow's face contorted, and the children who played the Orphans burst into laughter.

Sometimes the lyrics of the songs and the roles of the rehearsing pilgrims brought into focus their real-life burdens. At one rehearsal the Pilgrim of Sorrow broke into tears each time she attempted to sing the assigned song, "Nobody Knows the Trouble I've Seen." Later she explained that she had personal problems at home. It was easy to see how this *Heaven Bound* experience engulfed the players and the fans. The drama and its production were about hope, sharing, and caring. And it was the chemistry of the players' natural demeanor and real-life hardship that made the simple play so great.

After an exhausting rehearsal the players would return to their seats in the pews. The friction and tension of trying to perfect the performance would have bruised feelings and raised temperatures. In the therapeutic warmth of the final moments, however, everybody asked pardons of one another and then sang a closing song, "Blessed Be the Tie That Binds."

BEFORE A PERFORMANCE

In 1966 Reuben Bussey, who had come to Big Bethel as pastor two years before, had the church completely renovated to mark an important anniversary: one hundred years earlier, the congregation of newly freed slaves had voted to join the African Methodist Episcopal denomination. The entire building, everything downstairs and upstairs, looked new. When the *Heaven Bound* season started that fall, the players converted the downstairs Sunday school rooms into what they called the wardrobe room, a place where wings, crowns, and robes were made, and where women in the cast could leave their purses while performing in the play. Another little downstairs chamber, hidden behind the downstairs pulpit, was reserved as Satan's dressing room.

When a performance was about to begin, Florine Furlow would send a young male player into the dressing room to help Henry into his costume. Satan's wardrobe consisted of two sets of red satin tights, meticulously designed and laid out for him by Corinne Johnson, a young seamstress who worked with the wardrobe staff. Before putting them on, Henry inspected the tights with all the seriousness of a Hollywood star.

Since the church's new air-conditioning system did not reach the cramped room in the basement, Henry would soon begin perspiring in the heavy satin tights. Looking into his dressing mirror, he methodically applied his makeup,

Above: Costumed Angels emerging from the wardrobe room. *Right:* The Angels and Saints get ready for the grand procession to Heaven, singing "When the Saints Go Marching In."

a base of black and then a generous portion of what seemed to be petroleum jelly over that. "It's dangerous," he once said to his young helper, referring to his bouts with the Pilgrims in various acts of the play. "During one episode she struck me in a private place. I had to have surgery, afterwards," he confided. It was an injury Furlow never disclosed to the cast—not even to the culprit. Pulling the red cape over Furlow's shoulders and fastening it beneath his chin, the young helper swore never to tell Furlow's secret. Furlow's attention then turned to the show that was about to begin.

The last few moments before a performance were exhilarating and suspense-filled. Hurried last-minute preparations for the rest of the cast took place in the wardrobe room, where the doors were flung back furiously in the rush, letting out the happy sound of Angels oohing, aahing, and laughing while the wardrobe matrons attached their wings. Dressed in workers' smocks and with safety pins between their lips, the matrons of the wardrobe emerged from the wardrobe room in a flurry of activity. Milling about the Saints and Angels they inspected each costume closely. Florence Beasley, supervisor of the wardrobe, was an imposing presence: tall, dark, and stately, with silver hair and a full, confident voice. When she spoke, the players listened. When she advised, they took heed. Although she carefully controlled every detail of wings, robes, and crowns, her true value to the play lay in her mother wit, her maternal instinct, and her strong Christian presence. Beasley, a domestic worker for most of her life, was a bulwark in the church. As president of the church's Progressive Board, Beasley helped to raise thousands of dollars to bring the church through hard times. She also headed the Independent Daughters of Bethel, an offshoot of the Daughters of Bethel, also formed after the Civil War to care for the church's aged and sick members. Since the days of slavery, women like Beasley had modestly led the African American people and quietly inspired others to keep the faith.

In white robes and distinctive silver crowns that only the musicians wore, the three pianists—Florine Furlow, Harriette Enous, and Josephine Davis—hurried out of the wardrobe room and hastily wound their way up through the cavernous back staircase, which led to the sanctuary via a private passageway under the choir loft. Seated at their instruments a full thirty minutes before performance time, they played soft music for the many fans who arrived early to claim the best seats.

The early arrivals would pay close attention to the musicians, whose costumes gave the first clue about what was coming in the play. Furlow sat at the organ, and Davis took her place at the console piano. With roots running deep into the history and tradition of the church, the families of these two women had been anchored in Big Bethel since the 1880s. Enous, who played the concert grand piano, joined the church in 1927 and became part of the play in the late 1940s.

"They had *Heaven Bound* in their fingers," remarked one of the old Pilgrims about these women, all trained in music. Furlow, the eldest of the three, had studied the pipe organ at the Wesley Memorial Church Conservatory under the tutelage of the Atlanta city organist, Charles Sheldon. She had also studied with Spelman College's renowned music scholar Kemper Harrell and was one of the few pipe organists in the city who had been invited to play the elaborate Great Organ at Atlanta's Fox Theatre. Enous, a professional musician, held a graduate degree in piano and violin from Columbia University. And Josephine Davis, who played for social functions all over the city, grew up in a family of musicians and began studying music as a child.

As a prelude to the show, the musicians invariably began to play "Danny Boy" softly at precisely 8:15. Veteran members of the audience knew the tune as a signal that gave them a few minutes to settle their children and end their conversations. Downstairs, the cast also recognized the faint tune as the signal to join hands and form the traditional circle of prayer before lining up to go upstairs. The organist, who knew the prayer circle was forming downstairs, continued to play while Furlow, glistening in red satin tights, stood in the middle of the circle. It was old Satan himself who sent up the prayer for a successful performance.

GETTING READY FOR "THE KILL"

Twenty of the twenty-four Pilgrims in the play would be "saved" and would enter the white Pearly Gates shining above the pulpit. Peeping up into the sanctuary, the long line of Angels, Saints, and Pilgrims who waited in the rear stairwell for the show to start could hardly see the gates up in the choir-loft Heaven. When the lights dimmed the heavenly procession slowly made its way up into the packed sanctuary, where a resplendent Heaven was in full view. Then the real parade began. Lined with lights and filled with golden pipes, the towering archway on the west wall of the church made a stunning background for Heaven. The pipes were mounted on a wainscoted console from which hung sky blue construction paper with childlike depictions of clouds painted on it. Adorned with white covers, the neatly arranged seats in Heaven made a striking contrast against the sky blue paper. In a darkened church the chords of the organ and the splendor of the spotlights made Heaven a most desirable place to be.

But fate was not so kind to all the players. The impressive parade of Angels and Saints that marched proudly through the aisles toward Heaven left four

Pilgrims behind, never to catch up with the heavenly band. The play's authors sent the Wayward Girl, the Rich Man, the Hypocrite, and the older Gambler to that cramped cubbyhole reserved for the eternally damned in the northwest corner of the sanctuary—Hell. Missing out on an evening of blissful afterlife in Heaven, these four players found satisfaction in smaller things, like the flamboyance of their costumes and the laughter their acts drew from the audience.

ON WITH THE "HELLIONS"

Not very far into the drama, after three triumphant Pilgrims had already arrived in Heaven, the spotlight fell on the first Hell-bound Pilgrim: Doris Moreland Holiday, who staggered down the aisle in a stunning cocktail gown, with a cigarette hanging from her lips. A kind, loving woman, Doris threw kisses on Sunday mornings from her established seat in the pews. When trouble came in the lives of the church people, she went to their homes bringing cakes and comfort. But on the night of the play, Doris was the Wayward Girl, clutching a liquor bottle actually filled with tea. The Wayward Girl was a difficult role, previously played by some of the most talented woman in the church—Johnetta Parks, Bernice Gross, and Nellie Davis. The character, a dissolute drunkard, touched all those in the audience who knew the futility and dissipation of alcoholism. Although Doris lacked the strong singing voice of her predecessors, she was a fine actress.

The second Pilgrim to reach Hell was the Rich Man. By the mid-1960s, Leroy Irving played that role. A young schoolteacher, Irving always donned tails for his act in the play. He was seldom present at the regular Sunday morning worship services, and he often skipped rehearsals as well. But he always came through on the night of a performance. By tradition the Rich Man had always been a good singer, and Irving was no exception. He had one of the finest tenor voices anyone had ever heard, and the choir, thinning as its members grew old, needed a good strong tenor.

Louis Hawkins, the original Rich Man, was a stalwart Big Bethelite who had recently retired from the play. He had been a magnificent bass in the Celestial Choir. Like many of the older members, Hawkins had spent his working life in domestic service to a white family. The old master-servant order was fast coming to an end, however, as young African Americans in the sixties were finding such careers unacceptable. Nevertheless, Hawkins remained faithful to the last member of the white family employing him, and as church gossip had it, she left him the bulk of her large estate.

After the Rich Man came George Bolton and I, the Gamblers. Although Bolton was a veteran in the play, I was a neophyte, just starting in my role at the age of fifteen. Extremely nervous at first, I wondered how I had let Furlow coax me into such a thing. But I found myself standing in the north aisle of the church, waiting for my cue and facing Heaven, which I would never reach in my long *Heaven Bound* career.

With the chord that was our cue, my craps-shooting brother and I leaped down the aisle, into the spotlight, and into the roles of the Gamblers. Casting a pair of oversized dice in front of us, I forgot my nervousness and became a better actor than I had ever been in rehearsal. Once in front of the audience, I was transformed into a rotten, hard-headed sinner. I flashed my cash and threw the dice all around the chancel rail like a real pro. To my old Christian mother, I showed sharp annoyance as she pulled and tugged at me from behind and begged me to change my craps-shooting ways. Although all the Angels looked displeased, the old one perched on the northernmost tip of Heaven peered down at my evil activity with a cold, disdainful eye. She was Gabrielle Wise Dewberry, an angel in the play since its first performance in 1930. Her frown never let me forget the seriousness of my act.

After a good frolic with the dice in the spotlight, I eventually found myself isolated with Satan. By that time our Christian mother had lead my gambling brother out of my reach and on toward the Pearly Gates. Separated from my brother I stood motionless, spellbound by Satan. That instant, when time seemed to stop, Harriette Enous's fingers were rushing over the piano keyboard with a virtuosity that threatened to steal the show. I could feel the mood of the audience as it shifted from gay laughter to deep sadness. Evvie Smith Mabry, the Determined Soul, watched and waited from the rear of the sanctuary with the other players whose acts followed mine. Struck by the fate of the Gamblers, Mabry mumbled her reaction to herself: "One lost, the other saved—it makes me sad."

As a discreet signal for me to end my act, Satan flashed his eyes and I struck out running toward Hell. Around the altar and down the north side of the sanctuary, I would run, run, run into Hell! Fast on my trail was Furlow, old enough to be my grandfather but still a nimble Satan. From behind the screen, Robert Brown, an unseen fixture in Hell for many years, lit the brightly glowing hellfires to mark my arrival. Thunderous applause burst forth, and I did not again show my face until the end of the play.

FROM HELL, WITH LOVE

The Wayward Girl, whom I soon learned to call Doris, and the Rich Man were already in Hell when I arrived. Doris welcomed me, as she would for the next twenty-five years, with a warm hug, while the audience was still applauding

Doris Moreland Holiday as the Wayward Girl, a role she began playing in the early 1960s.

A red glow, occasional puffs of smoke, and a mural painted with images of the Devil and his imps set the scene for Hell.

The Rich Man, the Widow, and the Orphans.

my performance. Realizing that I was new in my role, she and the Rich Man encouraged me greatly with a large dose of praise for my performance. Even Satan would whisper a compliment after I was securely behind the Hell screen.

Once Satan was back on Life's Highway, however, the Rich Man, Doris, and I settled down to a whispered conversation. Waiting for the Hypocrite to arrive, we watched the remainder of the play through the cracks in the screen, a timeworn red mural painted with images of the Devil and his imps. We had to take care not to be seen peeping out, because the audience, especially the children, always seemed curious about our confinement behind the screen.

After wooing a Pilgrim, Satan would zoom into Hell with great speed. While catching his breath, he would examine closely the plastic apple, the parasol, or the beads he used as bait for his prey. With the props for his next act tucked neatly underneath his cape, he would streak out toward another Heaven-bound pilgrim. As the years passed, players behind the screen got a close-up view of the toll that Satan's theatrics were taking on the aging Furlow. Eventually a chair was set up in Hell so that he could rest during his brief stops there. After chasing the Pilgrims, he would flop down in the chair, almost collapsing from exhaustion.

The Rich Man was never a person of too many words—at least not in Hell. But Doris and I chatted throughout the performance and became great friends. She was a valuable asset to *Heaven Bound.* From her base as a stockroom supervisor at Rich's, Atlanta's largest department store, she worked hard for the play, often selling large blocks of *Heaven Bound* tickets to her many white friends at the store. Occasionally she persuaded her employer, Richard Rich, to come and see her perform at Big Bethel. Doris and a *Heaven Bound* stagehand, Willie Green, persuaded Rich's window dressers to donate the props for the play. From the store's stock of window decorations came the Pearly Gates, the plastic apple used by Satan to tempt Pilgrims, and the oversized dice used by the Gamblers. From Hell, we could barely see Doris's husband, Sam, who stood in front of the Pearly Gates as the latest Saint Peter. In his comfortable white tennis shoes, Sam routinely violated Heaven's dress code, which required dress shoes. But he and other Saints knew from experience that the two hours of standing required for the play could mean agony for tired feet in uncomfortable shoes.

Sam had a quirk about which he worried much but told only a few. He was uneasy because Doris always went to Hell in the play. He wanted her to come with him to Heaven at least once in her *Heaven Bound* career. But Doris never worried about Sam's idiosyncracy. She had a grand time going to Hell every year until her death, twenty-five years later.

THE HYPOCRITE—HELL'S DELIGHT

Daisy Payne Brown had become a smashing hit in the role she had played since 1942. The audience always began to laugh even before the spotlight could find her or the Scroll Reader could give her the cue. With the audience swinging right into her frivolous act, Brown, the Hypocrite, put her hands on her hips and strutted off down the aisle of the church, singing "I Shall Not Be Moved" in a soft equivocal tone, somewhere between piety and pretense. The pianists jazzed up the sacred song as Brown, charmed by Satan, meandered along, swaying rhythmically toward Heaven.

Aunt Daisy, as she preferred to be called, went back a good bit further than most of the players. Born in 1903, she was the same age as Henry Furlow and

The Hypocrite, Daisy Payne Brown, is ambivalent as Satan brandishes a bouquet of flowers, 1953.

Daisy Brown, the Hypocrite, with Henry Furlow, Satan, 1983.

The Hypocrite sings “King Jesus Is My Leader” but follows Satan.

DAY PRO
HYMNS

had weathered many a storm—the early loss of her mother, the Great Depression, and three marriages. She was a hard worker who faced a daunting daily routine to make a living. Leaving her southwest Atlanta home each morning before dawn, she walked three miles to a downtown bus stop. Catching a bus at 5:30 A.M., she arrived early—in time to get breakfast started—at the Veterans Administration Hospital, where she worked as a cook.

Nannie Braswell Coleman, who played the Pilgrim to Zion, made the Hypocrite's fiery red dress. Although the original Hypocrite wore white to indicate a feigned purity, the red dress trademarked the role in later years. And how Aunt Daisy could do the shimmy in that dress! She swung her skirts, doing exactly what the Scroll Reader deplored: "prancing with the Devil and posing as a child of God at one and the same time."

Henry Furlow never required Brown to go completely through her act in rehearsals. With hundreds of performances behind her, this gifted folk comic had already perfected the role. What had to be rehearsed were the stoic faces Furlow demanded of the Angels in Heaven when the Hypocrite, singing "I'm Sanctified and Holy," struck up a dance with Satan, or when she strolled up to the gate of Heaven and winked seductively at Saint Peter. Hopelessly funny, Brown never failed to break the icy composure of the Angels when Satan lured her from the steps leading up to the gate with a bouquet of wilted flowers.

Daisy Brown was a devout, fun-loving person whom everybody wanted to be near. Her jokes, which others tried desperately to remember for their own repertoires, made everyone roar with laughter at the choir's Christmas parties. But she was so effective as the Hypocrite because she knew the true purpose of her role—salvation, not humor.

"Make way for 'Aunt Daisy'!" someone would exclaim when Satan was chasing her toward Hell. And the sight of Daisy Brown running at full speed into Hell, her hands outstretched and her body leaning forward, was unforgettable. With a final desperate scream, she would hurl herself behind the screen—out of breath, of course, but obviously pleased with the thunderous ovation ringing in everyone's ears. "Let me rest my knees" she used to say. Then she knew just what to do for old Satan, her longstanding companion in the little den. With a towel she would wipe from his face the profuse perspiration, carefully leaving his makeup intact, while Doris, the Rich Man, and the Gambler looked on. Both Brown and Furlow, veterans in the play, looked tired, but triumphant.

The fight between Satan and the Soldier in the Army of the Lord was the climax of the play. With pitchfork spinning in hand, Furlow charged the Soldier with ferocity and speed, only to meet a determined sword and shield. Down the aisles and around the altar of the church Furlow fought vigorously. But the Soldier, still played masterfully by Waymon Bray, was undaunted. After all, Bray, now rotund and aging, had played her role as long as Furlow had played his—

since 1933. The loud clash of Satan's pitchfork with the Soldier's sword and shield could be heard throughout the church. Right up to the gate of Heaven, the fight continued until the Soldier delivered a lethal blow. So realistic was the final pain on Furlow's face that the audience remained breathless while he faltered for several seconds toward his climactic death. With Satan's final arrival in Hell, the Hell gang was complete.

Heaven Bound and Race

In the 1930s, *Heaven Bound* became known by several labels. Some called it a revival, a concert, or a pageant. Others thought of it as an opera, an allegory, or a morality play. The play also had a reputation as a box office hit. Besides all these identities, the play took on another: a bridge between black and white.

For much of its history *Heaven Bound* was a daring socioreligious experiment in interracial relations. The way in which it attracted and ministered to large numbers of white as well as black people was a rare and fascinating phenomenon in the South, especially in the days before integration. In the play blacks and whites found common ground, and the meeting of the races to see the performance at Big Bethel eventually became an annual Atlanta tradition.

Heaven Bound was also a pioneering effort in southern black theater. Nowhere had a drama written, directed, and produced by blacks claimed such widespread success. In its very first year, 1930, the play became a mature theatrical production attracting thousands of fans. This it accomplished four years before the historically black Atlanta University Summer Theatre came into existence. *Heaven Bound,* moreover, went in a radically new direction for black stage characters. The characters—the Pilgrims—were dignified. Never did Big Bethel's players speak in slang or shuffle or wear the degrading blackface and whitened lips typical of the old minstrel shows.

Although the play was first performed for an all-black audience, many of the actors soon invited their white employers. It was a smash hit with the whites. Again and again they came—thousands of them—to see the great play on Auburn Avenue. Some came to fill their spiritual cups, others simply to be entertained. Some came as scholars probing black music, and others as critics, both generous and condescending. They brought their children, who would grow up seeing and absorbing the play. Somehow, one got the feeling that the whites, who had so much more of everything on their side of the color line, came to *Heaven Bound* looking for something they could not get in their own world—something beyond art and entertainment. And somehow their tears,

White members of the audience react to the humor in the play.

their thunderous ovations, and their faithful return, year after year, seemed to imply that they got what they came for.

Heaven Bound's success in improving race relations was made possible by the tolerant racial climate prevailing in Atlanta even while segregation was still the law. Through the first half of the twentieth century, the state of Georgia compiled a horrible record of lynchings, disenfranchisement, and race-baited politics, and in 1906 Atlanta was the scene of one of the country's deadliest race riots. But Atlantans of both races worked hard over the years to improve relations. The city's forward-looking whites maintained open dialogues with a core of progressive blacks in the Auburn Avenue community and in the Atlanta University Center. In the 1940s increasing numbers of registered black voters became a political force respected by the whites in an atmosphere of moderation and peaceful coexistence. *Heaven Bound* was part of this positive trend in Atlanta's race relations.

Not only did Atlanta's whites flock to see *Heaven Bound* at Bethel Church, where they usually made up at least half of the audience, but the play went out to them. In the 1930s Big Bethel took its play to some of the oldest and most influential white churches in Atlanta: the First Presbyterian Church, Ponce de Leon Baptist Church, Peachtree Christian Church, North Avenue Presbyterian Church, and Saint Mark Methodist Church, among others. The play was also performed at several white schools and private clubs.

White Atlantans had always viewed Bethel Church as a sort of gateway into the black community, and they saw *Heaven Bound* as an open invitation to come in that gate. More than an opportunity to see a drama, the play was a chance for whites to come and feel the awesome power of the black worship experience, to cultivate ties in the black community, to form political alliances, and to see life from a black perspective. And how the whites responded! Big Bethel became a brokerage house where white politicians campaigned, consolidated political power, and struck deals. Choirs from the all-white Emory University came regularly to learn the unique cadence of the spirituals. White nurses and white medical interns also came from nearby Grady Hospital to worship with the black congregation and to make friends. Sunday-school children from Wesley Memorial Methodist Church, a church on the extreme western end—the white end—of Auburn Avenue, participated in an exchange program with Big Bethel's children.

But the peculiar role of the play in shaping race relations is rooted in traditions going back much further than Atlanta's comparatively progressive racial climate. The history of the A.M.E. Church, as well as the experience of the original slave congregation of Bethel Tabernacle, were part of the background. Born in Philadelphia out of a protest against racism, the A.M.E. Church at first maintained cautiously friendly relations with the white community. Richard Allen's plans to build a separate church for blacks were strongly opposed by many of the white Methodists. But several others aided Allen with their clout, their expertise, and their money. When the first church building was completed, Allen invited his white friends—wealthy Philadelphians—to celebrate the event with the new congregation. After the members served their guests dinner on the church grounds, the whites reciprocated by serving dinner to the blacks. Later many whites joined the A.M.E. Church. To the true African Methodists, cordiality was a simple Christian duty, as expressed in the motto of their church: God Our Father, Christ Our Redeemer, Man Our Brother.

A BACKGROUND OF WHITE PATERNALISM AND SHREWD ACQUIESCENCE

Blacks and whites had interacted at Bethel since the days of slavery, when the most positive race relations that could be enjoyed by the congregation were based on white paternalism. After the slaves who worshiped at the white Union Church petitioned their white owners for permission to form a separate congregation, the whites set aside seven hundred dollars—a considerable sum in those days—for the construction of a slave church. A wealthy Union Church member, L. P. Grant, allowed the slaves to build the church on his land. With 250 seats, a small balcony, and glass windows, the 600-square-foot Bethel Tabernacle was ready for Atlanta's slaves in 1855. Although the construction money gave out just before a steeple could be built, the determined slaves simply hung the bell they had already purchased on a scaffold outside and proceeded to occupy the little church. The independence the slave congregation enjoyed, however, did not remove it from the watchful eye of the whites. The law required whites to be present when sizable numbers of slaves gathered. The first ministers of Bethel Tabernacle, therefore, were white men—Issac Craverns and James B. Payne. When the black lay minister, Joseph Woods, was allowed to take over as pastor, John L. Rogers, a white man, regularly sat on the pulpit to ensure compliance with the law. On one occasion, when no white adults could come to the church to legalize a gathering of slaves, a black nursemaid is said to have brought in a white infant to fulfill the requirement.

Even after the institution of slavery fell, white paternalism—and the help, money, and protection that came with it—remained a critical factor in the growth and development of the congregation for at least seventy-five years. In 1868, when the members of Bethel Tabernacle built their second sanctuary, known as Old Bethel, whites, especially those visiting from the North, often worshiped in it and gave money to help pay for it. And the building of such an elaborate structure as the present Big Bethel, completed at the turn of the century, would not have been possible without white financial support: blacks simply did not have enough money for such a grand venture so soon after slavery.

The fire of 1923 was another occasion for white benevolence. Not long after the scorched crown of the east tower crashed to the ground, carrying with it the neon words "Jesus Saves," help was on the way. Rich's department store paid the cost of printing the church's appeals for help in the newspapers. A large white church downtown, the Baptist Tabernacle, held a benefit to raise money for Big Bethel. The event featured the band and glee club of Tuskegee Institute offering selections from the black Broadway hit *Shuffle Along*.

Several wealthy white individuals stepped forward to help rebuild the church, offering not just their money but their financial skills as well. A prominent white banker suggested the formation of the Big Bethel Concert Choir, a tour group that sang the spirituals to raise money. White bankers also restructured the church's debt several times to give the struggling congregation more time to pay off the mortgage contracted to rebuild the church.

The black parishioners not only understood white paternalism but knew exactly how to cultivate it. Just as the fledgling black colleges had sent their choirs singing the spirituals to wealthy whites around the country in the late 1800s, Big Bethel sent its choirs all over Atlanta doing the same in the 1920s and 1930s. On several occasions the choirs sang for groups of whites at Atlanta's grandiose Biltmore Hotel. There, after entering through rear entrances, kitchens, and stockrooms, the singers were met by guides who led them through ornate corridors and ballrooms to the private gatherings. The choirs took their music to private residences as well. On one occasion in the 1930s the choir sang at the estate of Julius DeGive, a socialite and the former owner of Atlanta's DeGive Opera House. The sweet sound of the slave music entranced the whites and opened their purses.

The benevolence of Big Bethel's white friends is not to be confused with egalitarianism. White loyalty to blacks was often based on ties that were strangely familial. It was not uncommon to find that several generations in a single white family had been served by several generations in a single black family. Some of *Heaven Bound*'s Angels, working as maids in private homes, had brought up whole families of white children, whom they loved dearly. Lena Cobb was one of those Angels. After she reached old age and retirement, her white family provided money for her care and well-being, bought a car for her, and paid for her clothes and medical care. And so it was between black domestics and their white families back in the old days.

CONTINUING THE OLD DIPLOMACY

Heaven Bound was conceived out of an urgent need to raise money. Just as remarkable as its fame and its tremendous biracial appeal was its success in employing the same brand of diplomacy used by earlier Big Bethelites to extract help from powerful whites. This strategy of shrewd acquiescence lulled the whites' uneasiness and enticed them into giving money to the church.

The antics of the capering, red-caped Satan, who danced with the Hypocrite and frolicked with the Gamblers, provided a comic counterpoint to the yearning of the Mother's Girl, the struggles of the Reformed Drunkard, and the desperate cries of lost souls in Hell. This delicate balance of lively action and pathos captivated the white people and made them reflect seriously. The very men and women who cleaned their homes, cultivated their gardens, cooked their meals, and reared their children were now ministering to their souls. It was a classic example of what Ralph McGill of the *Atlanta Constitution* called the black people's "moral indictment" of white southerners who discriminated against them. The deep sense of guilt felt by many of the wealthy whites as they watched the play often produced money and gifts for the church. The blacks, eager beneficiaries of this much-needed charity, showed surprise and pretended not to have known the effect the play would have on the whites.

The congregation was well situated to press Atlanta's whites for money and favors. Several of Big Bethel's members worked as domestic servants for some of the wealthiest whites in the South. From the kitchens of the mansions where they worked, an entire network of cooks and housekeepers set about urging their wealthy employers to come see the play. Emma Akers, an Angel, was the seamstress for the wife of Asa Candler, the founder of the Coca-Cola Company. And Mother Lou McNeal was the cook for John Slaton, a former governor of Georgia. Right next door to Slaton's estate was the residence of a prominent Atlanta lawyer and real estate magnate, Walter P. Andrews, whose cook was Bessie Jordan, another Big Bethelite. Julia Jackson was the maid for Robert Woodruff, president of the Coca-Cola Company, and Charlie Zanders, a Gambler in the play, was Woodruff's valet.

The fine reputation of the church's choirs and the curious loyalties between black domestics and their white employers got the job done. Atlanta's white aristocracy was well represented at *Heaven Bound* performances. Among the rich and powerful white families regularly seen at the play were the Havertys, owners of fine furniture galleries, and the Peters, wealthy investors in the cotton-textile industry and in railroads, whose family home, only a short distance from the church, was later converted to the Mansion, a renowned Atlanta restaurant. Also present in the audiences were Clark Howell, publisher of the *Atlanta Constitution,* and Richard Rich, the department store owner.

These prominent white Atlantans did more than patronize the play: they gave to the church and its members the influence and protection of their social rank, their political muscle, and their money. Some of them gave a specific gift as a remembrance of the donor or in honor of an employee who was a member of the church. The Peters family and the Havertys gave the iron gates and fence that enclosed the church. The hardwood floors in the sanctuary were a gift from the Candler family, and Richard Rich gave the green carpet. Sometimes gifts came in curious ways. More than once Charlie Zanders brought to the church fine wines from Robert Woodruff's cellar. Taking such liberties was looked on not as petty theft but as a privilege of being close to great wealth. The wine was blessed and given as the sacrament at Big Bethel's communion table.

Some donors, like Richard Rich, preferred to keep their gifts anonymous. In the 1950s, Louise Cummings, a lifelong member of the church, worked downtown as an elevator operator at the elite Commerce Club, where white businessmen made deals over lunch. Like most elevator operators, Cummings was considered "safe" by the whites, who continued their confidential talks after the elevator doors closed. There was a time, recalled Cummings, when all the whispered conversation around the club was speculation about the amount of money Dick Rich gave Bethel Church through a woman who worked in his store and served at his private parties. That woman, of course, was Doris Holiday, the Wayward Girl.

The way the black players plucked the heartstrings of white charity was neither fraudulent nor subservient. It was simply an effective combination of interpersonal skill and provocative theater aimed at reaching the conscience of a target audience. Many of the *Heaven Bound* players who affected whites so positively were in the vanguard of militant, church-sponsored social activist programs that worked for civil rights alongside the NAACP, the Urban League, and the Negro Voters League. *Heaven Bound* was just another tool Big Bethelites used to advance and protect the interests of the church and of the race. *Heaven Bound* continued to serve this function until the civil rights revolution of the 1960s yielded a whole new tool chest of protest techniques, political action, and other ways to bring about change.

Despite the whites' support for the church and their fondness for the play, the blacks dared not forget that whites generally deemed themselves superior. In the early days of the play, this attitude showed up in the reviews published by white newspapers and magazines. Though the reviews were mostly laudatory, they were also laced with racial stereotypes. An *Atlanta Journal* article covering a performance in 1931, for instance, referred to one black woman in the audience as "a beaming aunty" and to another as "a dusky damsel." *Theatre Guild* magazine described a predominantly black *Heaven Bound* audience in Savannah as "row on row of black faces, rotund, shining, eyeballs rolling."

White members of the audience held rapt by the performance.

For the favors they extended, the whites generally expected the blacks to "stay in their places." At the Atlanta Municipal Auditorium, at the Atlanta Theatre, and at other public places where the play was performed during the 1930s and 1940s, the races did not sit together. In those days seating was noticeably segregated, even at performances given at Big Bethel. The whites seated themselves in the forward section of the sanctuary. At first the black church officers winked at the practice, rationalizing it as the result of charging higher prices for preferred seats. Law, custom, and habit, however, had led whites to expect not only separate seating but the best seats in the house. The separate seating eventually became so distasteful that the church officers disallowed it. They adopted a policy of open seating, charging the same price for all tickets except children's.

Despite racist insults and southern white attitudes, the blacks remained shrewdly diplomatic, playing along and sometimes going all the way to the limit of their human dignity in humoring or entertaining the whites. This dubious diplomacy—shrewd acquiescence—kept much-needed money rolling into the church. The members well understood that white paternalism was vital to Big Bethel's survival.

BEYOND MONEY

Not gaining favors from the whites but the colorless business of soul saving was the ultimate objective of the play. In its simple way, the play took aim and struck the consciences of its viewers, regardless of race. Indeed, for two hours the play blended large numbers of people from all kinds of backgrounds. For this short time they all became a single fellowship of entranced mortals.

Although the play's message was universal and its drama enjoyed by all, the ultimate effect it had on the whites seemed to be different. The blacks viewers, who saw many of the players and heard some of the songs on Sunday mornings, looked forward to the play as an evening of fun and nostalgia as well as reverent reflection. Although enjoyable, the play to the blacks was a routine affair that lingered little into the days afterward. The whites, on the other hand, seemed more serious about it. They revered the Pilgrims and looked on the spectacular Satan with awe and amazement. The spirituals seemed to move them deeply, often sending them away contemplative and even a bit unsettled. "I am sure that the Spirituals of your race are much more beautiful than the religious songs of my race," wrote one of Henry Furlow's white fans after the close of a *Heaven Bound* season. The *Heaven Bound* singers, knowing the passions of the whites, sent them coded messages through the spirituals, just as the slaves had done in the antebellum South. "He sees all you do and hears all you say. . . . My Lord's a'writin all the time," warned one of the songs. The responses from white fans was sometimes dramatic, going beyond guilt and charity. "You don't know what you did to me," a white playgoer would say to this Pilgrim or that one, after seeing a performance. "You've converted me," another would say.

Ralph McGill described the beauty of spirituals as "haunting." He no doubt understood the power of the spirituals to shake the whites and strike universal chords. Perhaps that is why he recommended the play to his staff of young white reporters. "Go. You need to see it. . . . It's uniquely Atlanta," he instructed them.

BLACK PRIDE AND BLACK IDENTITY REVISITED

Because it drew audiences of different races and classes, *Heaven Bound* was a good vantage point from which to view the social activism and the shifting trends of the 1950s and 1960s. Before this period ended, the play itself underwent a social metamorphosis.

Beginning in the 1950s, race relations were redefined and redirected toward the goal of integration. White rejection and a resurgence of black pride, however, once again caused blacks to look inward and consider what it meant to be black. A powerful wave of collective black consciousness swept the country during the 1960s and gave birth to a proud new black identity. An emerging black theology made black dignity one of its fundamental premises. Some black scholars even pronounced the death of the old "Negro church," in which they said blacks had sought merely to emulate their white counterparts. The birth of the new "black church," a church summoned forth by Martin Luther King Jr. and empowered by his example of social action, was being proclaimed. Art and literature by blacks were also flowering, and a new black theater built on pioneering works like *Heaven Bound,* the coastal "Devil plays," and dramas presented on black college campuses. The worldwide African Methodist Episcopal Church was infused with this new cultural pride, which was later reflected in its bicentennial recommitment: "The A.M.E. church must be committed to identify itself with a value system which has grown out of the Black experience with God, and not the adaption of another culture. . . . The value system should interpret the intervention of God within the Black context and the historical pilgrimage of Black people."

The strong currents of ethnocentrism in the larger environment pervaded the thinking and attitudes of Big Bethel's younger *Heaven Bound* players during the 1960s. Like other young blacks, they grew almost as skeptical of the ways and customs of older blacks as the older blacks had been about the intentions of racist whites in the days of segregation. The young players sensed something anachronistic about the way the old play handled race matters, and they set out to put that something under a microscope. New civil rights laws promising a brighter, more secure future made it possible to avoid the domestic careers to which many of the old players had been confined. The young blacks could now start anew. Shrewd acquiescence, the tool of survival handed down by generations of older blacks from their segregated existence, was put on the shelf. Pride and the celebration of black culture became the major focus of the play.

The new pride was evident not only in the careers, in the lifestyles, and the thinking of the younger *Heaven Bound* players but on their faces, as well. The whitened theatrical faces and the straight hair that were part of the traditional costume of the Angels started to disappear. The Angels' black faces were unadulterated by the whitening powders and bleaching creams previously used by the older players. Many of Heaven's inhabitants stopped using their straightening combs and began to display, for the first time, the natural Afro hairstyle.

Even though changing race relations, new career opportunities, and a new black identity were permanently altering the social chemistry of the play, *Heaven Bound* quietly continued its mission of spreading goodwill among the races. In an article covering the 1971 opening performance of the play, the *Atlanta Constitution* reported that "by the time the celestial chorus reached the finale the overflow crowd of blacks and whites was exhibiting a spirit of euphoric brotherhood that would have made the angel Gabriel himself proud."

Commitment: The 1970s

From the beginning *Heaven Bound* tickets remained in very high demand. In 1971, when the *Atlanta Constitution* announced the 758th performance, the church claimed that more than one million tickets had been sold over the life of the play. Though only an estimate, the figure was credible in view of the large number of performances scheduled to raise money during the Depression. Hundreds of times during the 1930s and 1940s, *Heaven Bound* filled the church's two thousand seats, and several times it played to even larger crowds in the old Municipal Auditorium.

Despite facing many challenges since the old glory days, *Heaven Bound* held on to its immense popularity even into the 1970s. On performance nights, the cars of playgoers jammed Auburn Avenue and the streets around Big Bethel, while buses packed with *Heaven Bound* fans from Memphis, Nashville, Orlando, and other cities pulled up to the church's big stone steps. Several renovations had reduced the church's seating capacity to about sixteen hundred, but the fans continued to come, standing around the walls and even sitting on the window sills to see the play. Indeed, the play was the only event in Atlanta that could still fill a large church to capacity on Thursday and Friday nights.

Although the play maintained its popularity, Big Bethel's congregation continued to shrink, as did hundreds of black congregations throughout the country. The black church had ceased to be the refuge it had been during the earlier part of the century, when blacks were largely uneducated, disfranchised, and isolated from white society. Not only were blacks better assimilated into the general populace, but they were more involved in activities outside the church. Big Bethel's congregation was also affected by the continuing movement of businesses and residents out of the downtown corridor. This urban relocation, and the money it took with it, drained downtown Atlanta and the Auburn Avenue community of their vitality.

Sunday mornings inside Big Bethel revealed the unsettling signs of decline. The once-filled balcony was conspicuously empty, and the famous Big Bethel choirs, although still vibrant, were visibly smaller. To galvanize the choirs, Pastor L. J. Jones, who came to the church in 1977, organized the Mass Choir—a combination of all the choirs in the church singing together on the first Sunday of the month. Fortunately, most of the members who had moved to the west side of Atlanta journeyed back across town to Bethel on Sunday mornings. Otherwise the church might have ceased to exist.

For a while the Auburn Avenue churches tried to reverse the decline in the community. Big Bethel and Wheat Street churches built hundreds of low-income housing units and even developed commercial space for restaurants, laundries, and other small businesses on the avenue. But the exodus of businesses and middle-income residents from the downtown district continued. Although the Auburn Avenue churches, banks, and funeral parlors stayed put, the theaters, hotels, and finer restaurants disappeared. Even the schools closed. What had once been an oasis for more than 120 black-owned businesses was becoming a dry memory.

On the eastern end of the street was one notable exception to the general decay: the birth home and final resting place of Martin Luther King Jr., Auburn Avenue's most famous son. To reach this national shrine, tourists from all over the world traveled the final stretch of Auburn Avenue, ignoring the stench of stale beer exuding from the brothels and their shabby clientele. The exotic ambiance of this strip, once a part of the culture that nourished *Heaven Bound,* was gone.

The deteriorating neighborhood, the dwindling congregation, and the infirmity of the old players began to work on the play as rust corrodes metal. Not only had many of *Heaven Bound*'s patrons left the downtown community, but the cast, which at its height numbered more than a hundred voices, was now back down to about sixty. Several of the players, moreover, began to look a bit strained as they marched to the fast tempo of the *Heaven Bound* parade. They were getting old.

During these years of decline, Big Bethel relied, as it once again had to, on the commitment and steadfastness of its bedrock members to provide continuity in the life of the church. The *Heaven Bound* cast and production crew were the finest examples of dedicated church people. Unsung and often unidentified, they labored together every year, bringing the greatest pride to the smallest details of the play. To them, *Heaven Bound* was a personal ministry, a calling. Because they pulled together, the play would neither falter nor fail.

BEHIND THE SCENES

To kick off the production season, the *Heaven Bound* Committee began to meet at the end of the summer and continued to work for about two months, until the actual performances took place. Florine Furlow always served fried chicken and hot, homemade biscuits at the first meeting, which was usually held at the Furlows' home in the Collier Heights section of Atlanta. It would have been easier for the Furlows to have the meetings at the church, but they, like the rest of the congregants, knew that the strongest bonds were formed in the warmth and intimacy of the members' homes.

The pastor usually dropped by the meetings to bless the committee's plans. Jones also blessed the chicken and biscuits of which he liberally partook. But Jones, like his predecessors, quickly realized that *Heaven Bound* was a lay project, from the moment of its conception down to the most recent production, so he did not have a great deal to do with the details.

Henry Furlow chaired the meetings, and Cora Wofford, a small woman with wavy silver-blue hair, served as secretary. Wofford, who sang with the Babcock Gospel Choir, was pious and devout but could tell a surprisingly good joke and enjoyed a glass of wine in moments of relaxation. The wardrobe supervisor, Florence Beasley, opened the meetings with a stirring prayer, while others collected their thoughts for a successful production. After the prayer Beasley and her helpers gave an inventory of crowns, wings, and robes. The musicians, reviewing their own work, closely critiqued the music of the previous year's performance.

Also at the meetings was Julius Green, the young sailor who had become homesick on his battleship in the Pacific after spotting a *Heaven Bound* feature story in *Life* magazine. Thirty years later Green was taking care of some of the staging details of the production. Keeping the Pearly Gates painted and tucking the microphones and stage lights neatly behind the clouds were chores Green seemed to claim for himself. It was also Green who always affixed to the exterior of the church the frayed, timeworn *Heaven Bound* sign, the first public notice of the opening production season. Hundreds of *Heaven Bound* fans in the audiences recognized him as the man perched on the railing of the balcony, beaming the spotlight on Pilgrims as they made their appearances in the play.

L. C. Henderson and Mary Bentley, longtime church officers, came to the meetings with plans to get the tickets on the streets. In the years when the races were strictly segregated, whole books of tickets were sent for sale in the white community. Henderson, then the only black manager at the Georgia Power Company, bombarded that company's employees with tickets. Charlie Zanders, who had become a steward in the church, flooded his coworkers at Coca-Cola with tickets. But none of these officers could beat the record set by Lena Cobb back in the 1940s. In her job as a maid at Davison-Paxon department store, now Macy's, she once sold more than two hundred tickets to the whites who shopped there. Although the issue of ticket prices occasionally came up, the committee always voted to keep prices within the reach of the poorest

Ernestine Zanders, a Guardian Angel.

people in the community. During the Depression, many of their fellow black people could not have seen the play if the ticket prices had been too high.

Some of those who worked most effectively behind the scenes were not always present in the planning meetings. Ernestine Zanders, a Guardian Angel and the wife of Charlie Zanders, was such a worker. A favorite among the choir members, Ernestine often hosted lively holiday dinner parties for her beloved Choir Number One. Growing heavier and older, she gave up the role of guarding Heaven's gate—a role she had held for twenty-six years. Instead she took up the post of self-appointed marshal of the telephone. After the committee posted a rehearsal schedule, Ernestine took to the telephone lines. With her familiar telephone greeting, "Hey puddin'," she reminded—ordered—absolutely everyone who had a part in the play to come to the rehearsals and to be there on time.

The critical business of the meetings was the effect the dwindling congregation and the aging cast were having on the play. Furlow, as Satan, had been running in the aisles of the church for nearly forty years. Retired from his teaching career, he now had snow white hair, and he looked tired. The Hypocrite, the Striver, the Soldier, and several of the Saints and Angels were also becoming silver-haired veterans of the play. In 1972 Furlow announced in one of the meetings that he had chosen a young tenor, H. J. C. Hightower of Choir Number One, to become the third Satan in the forty-two-year history of the play. For the next two years Hightower alternated with Furlow in the starring role. After Hightower resigned in 1974, Furlow waited two years before choosing a young baritone, Harold Henderson, as the fourth Satan.

The business of the planning committee was also affected by demographic trends in Atlanta. Every year the play had to be advertised anew to the city's shifting populace. For this job the church relied primarily on the hundreds of willing members who still provided that most effective form of advertising—word of mouth. Furlow also reported to the committee that his old contacts at the newspapers and radio stations would be pressed once again for coverage. One particularly clever form of advertising, discovered by Furlow back in the 1950s, was *Two Bells,* a leaflet published by the Atlanta Transit Authority, the predecessor of Atlanta's modern rapid rail system. *Two Bells,* as Furlow predicted in the meetings, carried news of the play to thousands of Atlantans who rode the buses and trolley cars.

The aroma of Florine Furlow's fried chicken was always a welcome distraction from the business of the committee. In her self-effacing way, she slipped away from the meeting and into her kitchen, where she worked to have the biscuits just hot out of the oven when the meeting adjourned. Everything about the play was entrusted to church people like the Furlows, and they always came through—with good food, warm fellowship, and, invariably, a fine production.

Harold Henderson, a new Satan, joined the cast in 1976.

FAITHFUL OLD CHOIRS—MAINSTAY OF THE PLAY

Although *Heaven Bound* was always a churchwide project, it was the strength and resiliency of Big Bethel's choirs that gave the play sustained success. Now that the church population was getting smaller, the play depended on that strong and resilient fiber for its survival. While the planning committee covered the details of the production, the choirs, without any prodding from the pastor, made ready for rehearsals and moved ahead with the play.

The Harvard music historian Eileen Southern points to Philadelphia's mother Bethel A.M.E. Church as the place where, in 1841, a trained black choir was first introduced into an African American church. Almost sixty years later, in 1898, the first choir of Big Bethel was organized under the direction of Mollie McCree. Although that choir split into two choirs in 1918, the influence of organized choirs in Big Bethel shaped the church's history for an entire century.

Big Bethel's choirs, like black church choirs everywhere, always seemed to be institutions unto themselves. Often rivaling the "hallelujah" preacher for the center of attention on Sunday mornings, the "amen" choirs at Bethel liberated the tensions and lifted the resolve of the weary churchgoers. The choirs were powerful and prestigious. Not only did they sing to God for and with the people, but they also raised money to help the struggling congregation. In addition, black choirs were also revered because of the special role they traditionally played in the black community. Because of the restrictions of segregation, black musical talent was typically nurtured in church choirs. Indeed, some of the great musical talents of the race—Marian Anderson, Leontyne Price, Aretha Franklin, Mahalia Jackson—started out in the choirs of black churches.

It was a great privilege to be a member of one of Big Bethel's choirs. Carefully socializing members into their ranks, the choirs offered musical exposure, identity, and a social outlet. The choirs were tightly knit social units that reflected a cross-section of the community. Indeed, domestic workers and college professors sang side by side as comrades in a common cause.

Commitment was also a hallmark of the Bethel choirs. The Sunday morning choirs of the 1970s lasted through several generation of the families who joined them. Second-, third-, and even fourth-generation singers and players could be identified. The pianists held an even more impressive record of commitment and continuity in the choirs. Florine Furlow of Choir Number Two, Harriette Enous of Choir Number One, and Josephine Davis of the D. T. Babcock Gospel Chorus together had chalked up more than 170 combined years at the keyboards of the church, including 140 years in *Heaven Bound*.

Since that moment in 1918 when the Big Bethel Choir broke into two groups, healthy competition became a way of life for the Bethel choirs, especially for

Second- and third-generation players. From left, the Christian, Weymonn Carney, and the Gamblers, Gregory Coleman and Al Wise.

Choir Number One and Choir Number Two. "Number One's members really felt they were 'number one,'" recalled Evvie Mabry, who was a charter member of Number Two. Often citing the great play as evidence of their superiority, Number One members also boasted that they had sent some of their own to Warm Springs, Georgia, to sing for President Roosevelt in the 1930s.

But Number Two was a fierce competitor. Taking care to keep secret their calendar of engagements, Number Two's members enjoyed springing surprises on Number One. Some of the surprises, like the invitation to sing in the world premiere of *Gone with the Wind* in 1939, were astonishing coups. Number One's members must also have been a little envious, too, when Number Two was featured in a pops concert sponsored by the mayor of Atlanta, William Hartsfield, in the 1940s. The concert, presented at the Fox Theatre, attracted five thousand people.

The cause of excitement was not always competition between the choirs but sometimes hot temperaments within a choir. Pastor Harold Bearden recalled being summoned hurriedly to the choir room downstairs in the church, where a fight had broken out among members of the Gospel Chorus. Bearden found the choir's pianist, Josephine Davis, doing what she did best when tempers flared. Utterly unflustered, she was playing a soft piano tune that soon calmed the combatants as if nothing had happened at all.

During the 1970s, Big Bethel's Male Ensemble and its Babcock Gospel Chorus shrank to a small circle of people standing around the piano on Sunday mornings. And the modern version of the old Junior Choir—now called the H. I. Bearden Choir—was a small unreplenished group of teenagers headed for out-of-town colleges and other churches out of the Auburn Avenue vicinity. But the main choirs holding up the play, Number One and Number Two, remained steady during this period. Number One, once a strong choir, had recorded anthems in the early 1940s. After the chorister, Leslie Nolan, died in the 1970s, the old choir seemed to struggle at times, though even without a conductor, the group was still cohesive and could rally some fine talent when the occasion called for it. "Bread of Heaven," a powerful song kept in the choir's repertoire from many years past, was still a favorite that the congregation eagerly awaited after the sacrament was given on the first Sunday of the month.

Choir Number Two was a stable group, neither losing nor gaining many members during the 1970s. The Furlows led the choir as a team and were the foundation of the group. In the 1920s and 1930s, Number Two enchanted many white gatherings and radio audiences with the spirituals. With a full complement of voices, including some outstanding coloratura sopranos, Number Two was still singing the old slave songs as few other choirs could on Sunday mornings. Ralph Johnson, the tenor who played the Striver in the play, stirred even the coldest soul with his version of the spiritual "I Got a Crown in Glory." Anita

Glover, the schoolteacher who played the Mother's Girl, made the spirit soar with her lilting rendition of "Did Your Soul Git Happy When You Come Out De Wilderness."

Life in the choirs fostered strong mutual attachment among the members. At their "Mad-Hatter Teas," at holiday parties, and on leisure trips out of town they revealed the sharing and caring of a happy family. The choir members also supported each other in times of trouble. When a member of one choir died, the other choirs sang in the choir loft while members of the bereaved choir, clad in their robes, marched in the funeral procession with the family.

The solidarity of the choirs was the foundation of the play. On the night of a *Heaven Bound* performance, there was no Number One or Number Two choir—only the Celestial Choir. On that night, no hint of competition appeared, and all the cohesion and rich history, all the talent and stubborn resolve of both choirs were brought to bear in the play. What they lost in numbers over the years, they seemed to gain in courage and determination on performance night. The magnificent unity that showed in the performances kept the play on a higher plane—a plane where success was always more noble, more beautiful, more powerful than the sum of its parts.

At the Crossroads

THE RISE OF A NEW ORDER

By the 1980s conditions surrounding *Heaven Bound* had changed so dramatically that a real question arose whether it could ever reclaim the high position it had once held in Atlanta's religious and cultural life. *Heaven Bound* was caught up in the dynamics of a city in flux and a church in evolution. For many of the despairing old-timers, even faint hope for some kind of revival seemed at times extravagant.

The Auburn Avenue environment in the 1980s was very different from that of earlier years. Atlanta had become a city of global importance. Its airport was one of the world's largest and busiest. A new symphony hall and an art museum joined with libraries, sky-scraping hotels, schools, and grand convention facilities to give sophistication and vibrancy to the downtown district. Although Auburn Avenue was a shadowed part of this same district, the city government repeatedly postponed plans to revitalize it. During the *Heaven Bound* season thousands of the play's patrons got a first-hand look at the homeless people, the prostitutes, and the small-time drug pushers who milled about Auburn Avenue.

Inside, Big Bethel convulsed with changes brought on by Father Time and the new pastor, McKinley Young. Young had grown up in Bethel. After serving churches in other parts of the country, he returned home to an unenviable task: to join the church's glorious past with a future not yet charted. Young replenished the membership with young parishioners. He also envisioned a sweeping redefinition of the church's mission and with it a complete realignment of all the church's projects and organizations.

It was business as usual when *Heaven Bound* entered its fiftieth year. The play had not yet confronted all the changes soon to come under Young's administration. Now designated a national historic shrine, the old sanctuary continued to shelter Life's Highway in its aisles and a beautiful Heaven in its chancel. The timeless spirituals were still bringing the house down.

Although no special celebration marked the occasion, a typically huge crowd was on hand for the fiftieth-anniversary performance. The energetic new pastor and the forward-looking new bishop in the district brought a special sense of rejuvenation to those old players who were still performing. Also present, as usual, were the press corps, dignitaries, tourists, and first-time viewers, many of whom had recently moved to town. Emissaries from other churches came as always, asking for the coveted script. Only a few were aware that the only script consisted of the Scroll Reading and some scant notes made by Nellie Davis. Before the performance a man who identified himself as a televangelist with the Billy Graham group seriously advised putting the play on satellite television.

Amid the noisy audience and clattering cameras, the sacred old play went ahead with characteristic modesty, calming and charming its audience to tears and reflection. Although all but two of the original players were now dead, little had changed about the play in fifty years. The acts, the costumes, the set—all remained virtually the same. With their steps slowing and their backs sloping under the weight of the years, the three keyboard musicians made their way to their instruments, as they had done countless times. Carrying not a single sheet of music, they began to play softly the old tunes they now knew by heart.

Henry Furlow, after forty-seven years, was still playing a charming Satan, although with a lot less speed. The alternate Satan, Harold Henderson, had established himself with *Heaven Bound* audiences, after four years in the role. A seasoned actor, Henderson had performed in Scott Joplin's opera *Treemonisha* and in a local production of *Porgy and Bess.* Putting some of his own touches on his role, the new Satan tempted fans in the audience with real apples—"forbidden fruit"—which he distributed as part of his act. The anniversary performance seemed utterly normal in all respects—a full house, a standing ovation. To undiscerning eyes and ears, the changing church and the uncertain future of the play were not apparent. It seemed that *Heaven Bound* could last, undisturbed, for another fifty years.

Not very far into the 1980s, however, Young began to accelerate change at Big Bethel. After a long spell of concentrated attention to debts, renovations, and other internal affairs, the old church began once again to look outward to the plight of the community. With the same zealous energy that had built the great stone edifice and brought literacy and educational advancement to the slaves and their descendants, new ministries at Bethel started reaching out to community members who were hungry, without adequate clothing, or in prison.

At the same time, a wholly different class of members began to replace the church's old social order, which had centered on the large number of schoolteachers in the congregation. The new members were much more diverse, working in marketing, public relations, banking, real estate, as well as the traditional professions. Indeed, these newcomers were generally more affluent than any previous generation in the church. The new level of affluence seemed to point out a new direction for the church's financial future. Gone were the days when Bethel depended on the solicitations of members working in the mansions of white people.

The new Big Bethelites, moreover, were not terribly impressed with the cool, Europeanized behavior of the older members. Rather, these new members were more interested in a worship style that reflected their African roots and the spirit of the lively new black church that emerged during the 1960s. Another mark of the newcomers was their transience. Many of them stayed only a short while in Big Bethel before relocating to other cities affording new job opportunities. New career paths, jet-age transportation, and electronic communications kept their options open and lifestyles fleeting.

Several of the old organizations became fatalities of change at Big Bethel. First to expire were the old boards—those smaller groups in which individual members had always found their place in the large congregation. The boards had also been the principal engines of fund-raising for the church. During the 1980s, however, these old groups were not replenished when their members grew old. Young set up other groups—ad hoc "teams"—for fund-raising. For fellowship among the congregants, Young also seemed to favor the new couples and singles ministries, or the revitalized class leadership system, under which designated officers, called class leaders, maintained contact with a small number of congregants assigned to their care.

Probably the most profound changes at Big Bethel came about in the music program. The old mainstay choirs, Number One and Number Two, were collapsed into a single new choir, the Cathedral Choir. Young also removed the old musicians and installed a younger, nontraditional music staff, headed by a young minister of music, Vernon Jones. A newly established choir, the Voices of Inspiration, rode the crest of the wave of changes, eventually becoming a symbol of the church's new direction.

Some felt that the changes were too extreme. Never in anybody's memory had the church broken so completely with its traditions. Many of the members who were upsetting the balance were young, new in town, and vulnerable to an old fallacy of youthful thinking: "Everything starts with us!"

The future of *Heaven Bound,* long a part of the old, traditional Big Bethel, was unsettled. The church was in transition, and the old way of church life was struggling to continue. Amid the tension of the times, it remained to be seen what future awaited the play.

THE STRUGGLE BEGINS

The changes taking place at Big Bethel had far-reaching implications for *Heaven Bound.* Although the old generation managed to hold on to the play and to preserve it for a while, the future promised to be very different indeed. When the play was first conceived, former slaves were still a part of the congregation. Their hardships, their music, and their faith profoundly influenced the play, its authors, and its players. Indeed, slavery, Reconstruction, and the struggle for literacy were the backdrop to the original play. But the younger members of Big Bethel seemed far removed from the past. To many of them, the traditions and the history of the church and its play appeared to mean little.

The transient lifestyles of the newcomers presented acute challenges for *Heaven Bound.* It was difficult to work them into the play without abandoning the training system by which the play had been preserved from one generation to the next. Neophytes had always been required to grow slowly into the play, usually by spending several years singing in the Celestial Choir before claiming starring roles. Stationed in Heaven's choir loft, the trainees could observe every detail of the play and the leading parts to which they aspired. This slow teaching process was the very way the play had reached perfection.

The newcomers in the 1980s, however, were impatient with Big Bethel's old custom of gradual infiltration into the play. They operated in a fluid, ephemeral world in which time seemed always to be in short supply. The pace of modern life allowed the newcomers little opportunity to absorb and grow into *Heaven Bound.* Some, realizing that a long wait might deprive them of the limelight, started demanding leading roles immediately. Others, though content to wait and watch, raised other issues of time—suggesting, for example, that certain Pilgrims and spirituals be eliminated to shorten the play.

Although the old-timers resisted attempts to adjust the play, the forces of change were sometimes overwhelming. Several poorly trained new parishioners found their way into the play. Some of them had never seen a single performance and truly did not understand the play. Woefully ill-equipped, these players sought merely to make their characters funny. Others, forgetting cues and lyrics, had to ad-lib their performances.

Even when the new players worked hard and came to understand the play, some of them still had difficulty portraying the Pilgrims with the same depth and intensity projected by the older players. It seemed that affluence had removed them too far from the everyday hardships that guaranteed a gripping performance. One woman, the wife of a wealthy baseball player, was one of the new members vying for a leading role in the play. Although her contralto voice was the finest the church had heard in a while, she was instinctively rejected for such roles as the Burden Bearer or the impoverished Widow. It was not that rich people did not have problems—even serious problems. It was just that Furlow could not imagine that people who drove Mercedes Benzes could have the same kinds of problems that had moved the old Burden Bearers to sing convincingly "I'm Gonna Lay Down My Heavy Load." The woman was allowed to play the Christian (the mother of the Gamblers).

The performing old-timers were able to draw on lives spent closer to the line of survival. As the children of former slaves and survivors of the Great Depression, the old-timers had life itself as their school of drama. When they sang "Nobody Knows the Trouble I've Seen," the audience, knowing it was true, empathized with them.

COMPETITION

Another challenge for *Heaven Bound* came from the many activities crowding the church calendar during the fall of the year: the fall revival, the anniversary, the Lay Fellowship Banquet, and a feed-the-hungry ministry known as the Welcome Table. No longer was the play the single event around which all church activity revolved. *Heaven Bound* now had to compete with other events for time, space, and attention. The increased activity sometimes generated friction and rivalry between the "old crowd" and the new.

The new choir, the Voices of Inspiration, was at first reluctant to embrace *Heaven Bound.* These younger singers maintained that the old players were stubborn, unwilling to accept change or to share the limelight they had monopolized for so long. So the Voices, as they came to be known, concentrated on making their new Christmas Concert a stellar annual attraction. Besides, this new choir was throwing its support behind another Harlem Renaissance play that seemed to be shaping up for regular presentation in the church—James Weldon Johnson's *God's Trombones.*

Members of the Cathedral Choir, which included most of the *Heaven Bound* cast, viewed the presentation of *God's Trombones* as a deliberate challenge to their play. Because the new play attracted much smaller audiences than those typically drawn by *Heaven Bound,* the old guard viewed the whole *God's Trombones* effort as a failure. But if there was a contest, it was not over.

Another occasion for comparison presented itself when the two plays traveled to Savannah in 1983. *God's Trombones* was presented by Bethel's new Theater Guild at the Civic Center. *Heaven Bound* followed at the First African Baptist Church, the oldest black church on the continent. The state of Georgia paid all expenses for the *Heaven Bound* trip because it was presented as part of the 250th anniversary of the founding of the state. *God's Trombones* drew several hundred people to the Civic Center. *Heaven Bound* was a quick and easy sell-out in the twelve-hundred-seat Baptist church. Although crowds at the two performances were probably comparable, the old *Heaven Bound* cast claimed victory. Florine Furlow summed up their reaction: "We went down to Savannah and 'ate them up.'... Now, they'll come calling for 'Heaven Bound'... they'll come calling...."

The standoff between the choirs soon relaxed. As it happened, regular *Heaven Bound* rehearsals were scheduled on nights when the Voices also rehearsed at the church. The *Heaven Bound* cast and the Voices took the opportunity to study each other, albeit from opposite corners of the large sanctuary. Young members of the Voices could hear the old *Heaven Bound* music and, out of the corners of their eyes, could see the old actors rehearsing the dramatic parts. Curiosity led a few of them to wander over to the *Heaven Bound* camp, where they observed the Pilgrims close up. This trickling of newcomers into *Heaven Bound* territory was the beginning of the long and sometimes painful transition from the domination of the old players to the installation of the new generation.

The old-timers, though possessive of their play, were not fools. Time was running out, and the newcomers, different though they were, seemed to be the only hope for the play's future. To convert them, not fight them, seemed the wiser course. Several of the old players began trying to help the newcomers work their way into the play. Florine Furlow, for example, gingerly approached each new player, offering her help along with a pamphlet giving a short history of the play. And Ralph Johnson, the longtime Striver, took many new auditioners aside for private instructions. People like Furlow and Johnson disarmed the newcomers and dispelled the notion that *Heaven Bound* old-timers were hostile. The door opened, and slowly but surely, new faces could be found buried in old song sheets.

DOWN WITH THE SPIRITUALS, UP WITH GOSPEL

With the 1970s and 1980s came a trend toward a different kind of music in black churches around the country. "Contemporary gospel," usually called "gospel," was becoming the new sacred music of choice for the many young blacks returning to the churches after a decade of apathy. Gospel caught on not only in the churches but on college campuses, in the recording industry, and in communities all over. Such religious dramas as *Mama, I Want to Sing* and *The Gospel at Colonnus* swept the country with the power of the gospel sound. This wave of high-energy music rolled into Big Bethel, threatening to uproot the spirituals that had become the centerpiece in the church's worship services as well as in the play.

Popularized in the 1920s by Thomas Dorsey, a Georgian, gospel music from its very beginning emphasized drums, tambourines, pitch, and secular blues-like sound. As a trend, Dorsey's gospel music was too new to catch the attention of those who wrote *Heaven Bound.* The lively song "Moving Up the King's Highway" is the closest thing to gospel music in the play. The gust of demand for contemporary gospel seemed an ill wind to Big Bethel's traditional members. And the suggestion that contemporary gospel selections might be used to update the play caused consternation among the old players.

Like other features of church life, sacred music seemed to enjoy no immunity from the whims of taste and style. What was fashionable during one period did not necessarily suit the fancies of another time. In the earliest years of African Methodism, the spirituals were disdained. Even after Fisk University choirs "legitimated" the spirituals in the nineteenth century, securing their place as a respected genre of music, many middle-class black worshipers remained hesitant about them.

An undeclared debate over the kind of sacred music appropriate for Big Bethel took shape in the 1980s. The elimination of the old musicians and the merger of the old choirs into the Cathedral Choir seemed to set the stage. Although Sunday-morning bulletins continued to list a balanced menu of hymns, anthems, and spirituals, these genres were sung less and less by the choirs. The new musicians were, strangely, the antithesis of the old. Although both were formidably well trained and capable of performing all types of music, their musical preferences seemed diametrically opposed. Just as the Furlows chose anthems and spirituals for Choir Number Two, the new musicians had a definite bent toward contemporary gospel. Indeed, the gospel motif became more and more prominent in the music of the worship service as the old musicians were gradually replaced.

The animation of gospel music seemed to please the younger, more Afrocentric Big Bethelites. Its emotional appeal reflected the strong African tradition of the ring shouts, hand clapping, and call-and-response handed down from the "invisible" slave church. The gospel sound also seemed to hasten the return of shouting in the worship services. Sometimes the services became so spirited that members left their seats and skipped around shouting from one end of the church to the other.

Many of the older members still clung to traditional patterns of behavior. To them the new music sounded too rowdy and too much like the blues to be considered sacred. They doubted that the spirited clapping and swaying of the younger choir were spontaneous reactions to the Holy Spirit. The drums, tambourines, and high-pitched, repetitive songs were not a joyful noise—they were just noise, sometimes untempered by any meaningful content. The younger members considered these old-timers staid, stubborn, and shamefully reluctant to clap hands, say "amen," or otherwise acknowledge God aloud during worship.

Fractures in the African American experience seemed responsible for this conflict in black religious life. Besides the usual differences between generations, blacks were divided in their opinions about roots, class, identity, and direction. These divisions, uncommon in earlier generations, seemed to obscure a heavenly vision that was once clear to all. Inside Big Bethel the old and the new collided head-on, each camp arguing in effect that God could be invoked in only one musical genre. The view that everyone's spiritual palate might be satisfied by singing a variety of music was not popular with the old or the young. That the ways to God might be countless and diverse was a position with little appeal.

Many of the members viewed the shift in emphasis from spirituals to gospel as an uneven exchange. Old-timers looked back nostalgically on the days when the old choirs struck up foot-thumping renditions of "Just Come from the Fountain," "Plenty Good Room," or "I Got a Crown in Glory." The spirituals had been vitally important throughout the history of Big Bethel. Indeed, from the time the Big Bethel Choir was organized until the demise of Number One and Number Two, the fame and glory of the church's choirs had been built on the spirituals. For much of that time, so had the church's financial security.

The spirituals also linked Big Bethel's present with its past. The old songs preserved the religion of the slaves and their faith that God would deliver them to a better life on earth as well as in Heaven. The spirituals also captured the genius of the slaves—their gifts of memory and poetic rhyming, and their ability to transform biblical stories and hymns into rhythm and song. Now *Heaven Bound,* with its repertory of sixteen spirituals, had become the only event in the church that still celebrated the old slave songs as treasures of the past.

SURVIVING A BAD SLUMP

Despite the deep, pervasive changes at Big Bethel, *Heaven Bound* remained reasonably healthy for a while. A trip to Savannah, the first time in many years that the choir had taken the play on the road, was reminiscent of the tours of fifty years earlier. The tales, jokes, and songs shared by the cast on the two buses rekindled some of the camaraderie and esprit de corps that had bonded the touring players during the Depression.

Although the trip had lifted the spirits of the *Heaven Bound* cast, its effect was short-lived. The old choirs soon resumed their downward slide in size and morale. In 1984, only a year after the Savannah triumph, the play sank to the lowest point in its long history. Only about two hundred people, the smallest crowd in anyone's memory, came—probably out of sheer habit—to see the play. The huge sanctuary was virtually empty.

The problem could be traced to two sources. First, the older choir members had not welcomed the merger of Number One and Number Two into the Cathedral Choir. During the *Heaven Bound* production season these old singers were disgruntled, and they did not promote the play by word of mouth with their usual enthusiasm. The other problem was Henry Furlow's advancing years. Now reaching his eighties, he was simply worn out, too feeble to press his many contacts—broadcasters and newspaper columnists—into service. At this low point in the play's history, many of the newcomers felt the play's time had come. One of the new musicians in the church came to a meeting of *Heaven Bound* old-timers and pronounced the play dead.

After the unhappy season closed, Furlow called me to his home one evening for an assessment. Our relationship had mellowed by that time. Furlow had initiated me into the Masonic Lodge, and I had become his lawyer. As we sat chatting by the fire, he asked me to take his place as Satan and as director of the play. He was tired. Florine, who obviously had discussed the matter with him earlier, nodded her approval as he talked. The word was out that the younger Satan, Harold Henderson, was about to resign, and Furlow was too weak to pick up the slack. My reaction to Furlow's request was pure shock. Although I had entertained some idea about helping with the promotion of the play, I had never imagined myself in Satan's red satin tights. Furthermore, I had never been a member of any choir and possessed none of the vocal or dramatic talent that would put me in the class with Furlow. I had to think about it, pray about it, and then think and pray some more.

Of the many hats Furlow had worn in the play—soloist, producer, director, Satan—I decided to try only one: producer. With the pastor's approval, I immediately set about recruiting a director, someone who had a feel for the pageant and for the people in it, someone who could be a broker between the new members and the old ones and could inspire both. Above all, the new director had to be someone whom Furlow trusted. That person turned out to be Jo Anne Bearden Vickers, the daughter of former pastor Harold Bearden, who was now a bishop. Like the Furlows, Vickers was a teacher and a member of Choir Number Two. Also, she had been an Angel in the play since the early 1950s. Furlow was pleased.

My next challenge was to find some new Satans. The church had suddenly recognized a danger that had existed for too many years: there were not enough

Satans for the play. Furlow's obvious infirmity had made people wonder for the first time "What if no Furlow?" After much speculation, everyone agreed that the devilish, cavalier Roland Young, the pastor's brother, should become the fifth Satan. Furlow approved.

The season leading up to the 1985 performance was filled with uncertainty and suspense. No one knew for sure whether the play was still alive. But the cast worked enthusiastically, and as opening night approached everything was almost ready. Wendall Whalum, a music scholar from nearby Morehouse College, had worked with the choirs and had brought out their very best sound. Vickers did an admirable job of bringing the new and old players together. The old Moller pipe organ, which had been out of the church more than a year for an overhaul, was scheduled to be back in place, with even more ranks of pipes. As for me, I had finally come to the end of a long list of chores assigned to me by Furlow. After making every single media contact he had given me, I was exhausted, but to my delight, several radio stations and newspapers responded with lively promotional pieces about the play.

It worked! The crowds packed the church to overflowing. Even the windowsills were filled with eager new *Heaven Bound* fans. The fire marshall—that happiest sign of *Heaven Bound* success—was there once again, as he had been in earlier years, to limit admission to the sanctuary. Although the pipe organ did not come back in time, the audience rocked and swayed with the singing of the spirituals and gave deafening ovations. A third night's performance had to be scheduled to accommodate those who had been turned away at the door.

The pastor who had ushered in one change after another in the old church had seen the wisdom of leaving *Heaven Bound* intact. The *New York Times,* in a five-column article, hailed the performance as "one of Atlanta's most enduring traditions." The church's new members were amazed and awestruck at the power of the play and the size of the crowds it commanded. And the old-timers—well, they were just glad the play was alive and well!

Truly Heaven Bound

SKETCHES OF A PROUD CHURCH HISTORY

The four church buildings occupied by the congregation in its 140 years were all just a short walk from one another. The old Union Church, where the ancestors of Big Bethel's members worshiped as slaves in a white congregation, was in downtown Atlanta, on Peachtree Street. Established around 1847, the little clapboard church was Atlanta's first. In the spot where Union Church once stood, towering columns of glass and steel now rise into the endless blue, leaving no trace of the past. Just blocks away from Peachtree Street was Jenkins Street, where the slaves built their own church, Bethel Tabernacle, with money given to them by the whites. Under its present-day name, Auditorium Way, Jenkins Street now skirts the limestone halls of Georgia State University.

Auburn Avenue, site of both Old Bethel and Big Bethel, is also in the central downtown district, but when the slaves were still worshiping in the Union Church, the nearby street that one day became a major black commercial center was no more than a marshy thicket. Before the close of the nineteenth century, horses trotted along the street, pulling buggies of worshipers up to Big Bethel's steps. By the 1920s the ringing of streetcar bells had replaced the beat of the horses' hooves. And by the 1950s and 1960s, the music and pageantry of colorful Masonic parades epitomized the bustling life of Sweet Auburn.

The 1980s brought quite a different repertoire of sounds to Auburn Avenue. Atlanta now suffered from the stresses of a modern metropolis—congestion, crime, homelessness, and a shifting population. While McKinley Young thundered from Big Bethel's pulpit on Sunday mornings, howling ambulances and speeding cars whistled past on the nearby superhighway. Gone were the days when Big Bethel ministered to a warm, stable neighborhood nestled at the heart of a thriving commercial center. And gone were the days when most of the country's blacks lead a church-centered, Heaven-focused lifestyle.

Despite all the changes sweeping across the twentieth century, some things did remain the same. Big Bethel and all it stood for were still there. And motorists streaking along the highway could still see on the skyline the old cross-crowned steeple bearing the blue neon message seen by thousands of Atlantans through the years—"Jesus Saves."

The original slave congregation would have been proud of the twentieth-century Big Bethel. The massive gray stone church on Auburn Avenue became a bulwark in the community and a unique symbol of progress for blacks. In Georgia, Big Bethel was the flagship church of the denomination, leading more than five hundred A.M.E. congregations with more than eighty thousand members. Bethel gave the city its first black congregation, its first school for black children, and a respected liberal arts college. F. J. Peck, one of the church's early pastors, brought black Masonry to the South soon after the Civil War. The secret fraternal order that he founded in Atlanta, the Prince Hall Free and Accepted Masons, was one of the rare centers outside the church where black men could organize themselves into social units sponsoring character-building programs and civic campaigns. The Daughters of Bethel was one of the earliest examples of economic cooperation among blacks. Long before the days of Social Security, the Daughters cared for the sick and aged members and buried the dead. A safe harbor for political meetings and civil-rights strategy sessions, Big Bethel was a sort of headquarters for monitoring the affairs of the race. In the days before southern convention facilities became integrated, several of the nation's largest black organizations, including the National Urban League and Alpha Phi Alpha fraternity, held their national conventions in Big Bethel's large auditorium. Leaders from all walks of life relished the chance to speak at the venerable church. At the turn of the century members heard Booker T. Washington, founder of Tuskegee Institute and leading race diplomat of his time. President William Howard Taft spoke there in 1911, and Marcus Garvey, the pan-Africanist, in 1917. During the 1920s, Madame C. J. Walker, a manufacturer of cosmetics who was said to be the first black woman to become a millionaire, spoke from Bethel's pulpit, as did Mary McLeod Bethune in 1937, congressmen, mayors, and other high-ranking government officials over the years.

As the century came to a close, several other local black congregations had already grown larger than Big Bethel's flock. But the long years of leadership provided by the church somehow kept its pulpit respected as a gateway into the black community and a national and international forum. Presidential candidates—Jimmy Carter in 1970 and Bill Clinton in 1992—came to woo the black vote. And Nelson Mandela, the prime mover in the South African revolution, pleaded the case against apartheid from Big Bethel in 1990.

In this star-spangled church history *Heaven Bound* rose to a lofty place. A beacon for thousands of hungry souls, the play became a symbol of black literacy in the new century and a vessel of goodwill among the races. Through the Great Depression and the war years, through the restlessness of the 1960s, and the inner-city decline of the 1970s, the message of the play was the very witness of Big Bethel Church. The bright glow of this simple message—that good will ultimately triumph over evil, hope over despair, Heaven over Hell—shone through the vicissitudes of the church's history, making the play the pride and joy, the crown jewel, of the flock.

The sixty-year code of silence observed by the old-timers to protect the play from imitators succeeded surprisingly well. Although many spies took back to their churches bits and pieces of *Heaven Bound,* not a single church managed to duplicate it. Unlike other Big Bethel pageants, such as *The Wedding of Roses* or *The Parade of States, Heaven Bound* did not end up on the signboards of other churches. After the near collapse of the play in the 1980s, some members questioned whether it had been wise to link it so closely to the life and evolution of a single congregation, thus shutting it off from the church at large and from the world of the formal theater.

The silence surrounding *Heaven Bound* in earlier years caused still other problems. Scholars' attempts to clarify the play's history were deliberately foiled by older Big Bethelites who sincerely believed they were protecting the play from intruders. Sometimes their pleas of ignorance and their misleading answers resulted in the publication of incomplete or inaccurate information. None of the scholarly reports, for example, seemed able to distinguish which parts of the play belonged to each of its warring coauthors. The articles also missed the mark in trying to tie *Heaven Bound* to John Bunyan's *Pilgrim's Progress* or to the Devil plays of the Georgia seacoast. Although the conspiracy of silence and deliberate confusion continued for many years, the true story of the play's origin did eventually come to light. As the old conspirators died, interest in guarding once-precious secrets began to wane. Then, and only then, did facts about the authors and their work begin to creep into the brochures distributed at the annual performances.

EXIT A GENERATION

Although *Heaven Bound* had highlighted an entire era in the church's history, it seemed to mark a closing of that era as the 1980s drew to an end. The end was approaching, not the end of the play but the end of the generation that created and nurtured it. The style of preserving, performing, and producing the play was about to change profoundly. No longer the center of a thriving neighborhood, Big Bethel was now a commuter church in a depressed downtown area. Old attitudes about race, tradition, church music, and "good religion"—all essential ingredients in the original *Heaven Bound*—were now changed. The next years in the new Big Bethel continued to be a time of uncertain transition for the play.

Although the old mainstay choirs, Number One and Number Two, were a thing of the past, the 1980s closed with a few promising signs. Several young players were enlisted to fill out the ranks of the cast and choir. Daisy Lowe, a new Pilgrim to the Promised Land, easily drew the audience into the hand-clapping rhythm of her solo, "Come and Go." Joyce Young, a versatile vocalist, made an impressive Mother's Girl, and after Roland Young's brief tenure in the role, James Maddox showed great promise as the sixth Satan. The new church organist, Philip Skerrett, and Emma Scott, an old Bethelite but a new pianist in the play, busied themselves learning the music. Furthermore, the new McKinley Young Community Choir, named after the pastor, was sending its best voices into the play.

The arrival of so many new auditioners and players in the 1980s was a signal to the beleaguered *Heaven Bound* veterans that their generation's work was coming to an end. An increasing number of them were becoming feeble and were pulling back from the roles. Daisy Payne Brown found that her "legs gave out," just short of her fiftieth year in the play. Waymon Bray, the Soldier since 1933, was confined to a convalescent home. Too feeble to join the procession when the Saints came marching in on performance nights, some of the old Angels quietly left their posts. Others, still clinging to the play, hobbled up into the choir loft Heaven to claim their seats before the Heavenly Band arrived.

Some of the longtime players had died—Gabrielle Dewberry, one of the original Angels; Anita Glover, the marvelous soprano who had played the Mother's Girl; Ophelia Wilson, the longtime Guardian Angel; and Robert Brown, who had lighted Hell's fires for as long as anybody could remember. The death of Doris Holiday in 1988 was especially painful for me. For twenty-five years, she had been my companion behind the Hell screen. In that cramped space, we had laughed together and whispered to one another our thoughts about the play. Sometimes, in our hushed chit-chat, we seemed to solve the problems of the world right there in Hell. How well I remember our huddled faces peeping through a tiny hole in the screen to glimpse our favorite acts in the play. Doris's grieving husband, Sam, could not bring himself to play Saint Peter again.

The death of the old players, one-by-one, eventually left only one survivor from the original cast, Esther Wright McDonald. McDonald's life spanned the entire history of the play. Barely a teenager when the church caught fire in 1923, she was in the cast of the first run of *Heaven Bound* seven years later. "We made good money, enough to buy us some new choir robes," recalled McDonald, measuring the success of the first show. Through sixty years and hundreds of performances, she appeared in all but one, when she decided to watch *Heaven Bound* from the audience to see for herself "what all the people were making such a fuss about." In her old age McDonald talked of a bright future for the play—a future she knew she probably would not see.

Above: Jackie Green, a new Hypocrite, trained by Daisy Brown, the long-time Hypocrite. *Below:* The Pilgrim of Sorrow, Patricia Cockburn, followed by Satan, played by James Maddox.

Above: Fred Brown, a new Preacher, pushes Satan, James Maddox, over the altar rail. *Right:* Esther Wright McDonald, the last surviving member of the original cast.

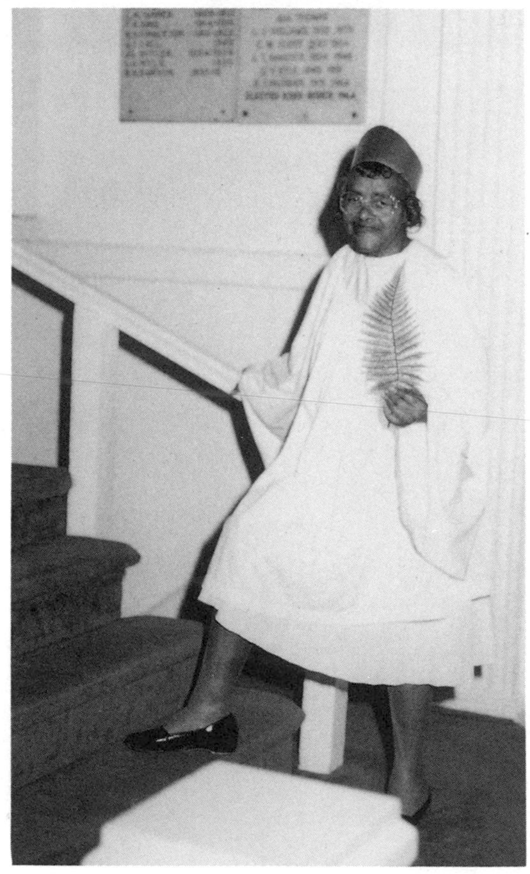

Although every year brought eager new faces in the *Heaven Bound* audiences, many of the old fans, loyal through several decades, kept coming. Never was there a more loyal supporter than Celestine Sibley, an extraordinary friend to the play since 1953. "I have to confess," she once wrote, "that it's the simplicity of the story, the wonderful cast of fumbling, striving human beings, . . . that have kept me going back and back again to Big Bethel." Her autumn columns in the *Atlanta Constitution* spread news of the play all over the South. Many times, readers of her column helped to fill the large church to capacity.

Once, in the fall of 1988, Sibley had brought her dying husband to see a rehearsal. After sitting through much of the long practice, she asked that someone sing her favorite spiritual, "Steal Away," before she had to leave to take her husband home. Nannie Coleman, the latest Pilgrim to Zion, rose to sing the old slave song. Coleman was at home with the spirituals. Like several members of the choir, she had spent her early childhood in the countryside with grandparents who had been slaves, and she sang with a deep sense of continuity with the past. "A wondrous soprano . . . tears sprang to my eyes," Sibley wrote in her column a week later. Listening to "Steal Away" also reminded Sibley of an interview she had done with the renowned baritone Roland Hayes. Hayes had explained to her the meaning of the spiritual: the slaves actually stole away to the backwoods and plantation praise houses to worship the God who would deliver them. Sibley wrote that the spirituals she listened to at the rehearsal refreshed childhood memories of black music she had heard in southern Alabama: "I grew up where spirituals were not just church songs but eased work days." The *Heaven Bound* choir later made Sibley an honorary Angel.

Many ingredients had combined to make the play great: the genius of the authors, the daring of the congregation, the richness of Auburn Avenue culture. But the one magic ingredient that made the drama so convincing was the faith—the real bedrock faith—with which the sturdy old Pilgrims, Angels, and Saints looked beyond death to a real reward in a real Heaven. It was the same faith, immutable and complete, that gave vision to the slaves and guided them and their children and grandchildren into the twentieth century.

This remarkable faith shone in the courage of two old *Heaven Bound* warriors facing death. To Henry and Florine Furlow, death was but a brief stop, an incidental point, in the continuing drama of their Heaven-bound journey. The old Satan himself had said in 1978, "I expect to go to heaven. I try to live in a way so that when my days on this earth are ended, I can go there without any difficulty."

The Furlows were well into their eighties. Henry Furlow's gait had already begun to slow down in the early 1980s. By 1985 he faltered and seemed off balance. His memory was failing, too. Florine Furlow, although still mentally sharp, was also showing the wear and tear of the years. Her sight was deteriorating and the characteristic energy in her step was gradually leaving. As their health failed, the congregation began to pay tribute to them for their long years of service to the church. All the parishioners gathered at a huge church banquet to pay homage to their outstanding work in the choirs and in the play. An annual organ recital was named in honor of Florine Furlow and Harriette Enous, and eventually a new choir was named the H. J. Furlow–Florine Dyer Furlow Choir.

Despite the accolades, the Big Bethel Church of the 1980s became a strange place to the Furlows. They no longer sang or played instruments there. Most of the anthems and spirituals they had taught the choirs for half a century had succumbed to the new gospel sound. Furthermore, new members from other localities were rapidly changing the face of the congregation. Although Florine Furlow occasionally worried aloud that the old members were becoming mere "furniture" in the changing church, she took a philosophical viewpoint. "Nothing is permanent but change itself," she often said.

In spring of 1986 Florine Furlow summoned me and the former pastor Reuben Bussey to join her beside her husband's sickbed. A master of euphemisms, she avoided ominous words like *death* or *cancer.* After talking softly with his wife about "a few problems that hadn't been solved," Furlow focused his eyes with an eerie sharpness and raised his trembling head from the pillow. "The best is yet to come," he said firmly. "The best is yet to come." He died in August 1986.

To mourn his passing, an enormous crowd of schoolteachers and former students, fellow Masons and fraternity brothers filed into Big Bethel along with hundreds of Big Bethelites and *Heaven Bound* fans. Florine Furlow, calmly and resolutely, assured their friends, "He's smiling with the other saints of *Heaven Bound.*" The long flight of stairs that Florine Furlow had climbed into Big Bethel since the dawn of the century was getting a bit steep for her. In her niece's home, where she would spend her last days, she would sometimes voice her reflections about her own fate as well as the fate of the play. "I have to face it . . . I'm ill and I won't be around very long . . . but I know *Heaven Bound* will make it . . . we pray it through," she used to say in a fading but firm whisper. In the fall of 1986 she played the piano for one more performance of *Heaven Bound.* The eye of the public and the electricity of the performance charged her with strength for this final show, the last two hours of a career spanning almost eighty years at the keyboards of Big Bethel. The fans, especially the old-timers accustomed to seeing her at the piano, smiled broadly when she appeared. Like her late husband, Florine Dyer Furlow made an indelible imprint on *Heaven Bound.*

The Furlow's deaths left a definite vacuum in the play. Nobody could pull the cast and crew together as they could. They had understood the history of the church and the personality of its congregation. They had taught and disciplined the singers and the players. Their long partnership—a union of her music and his drama—had been a pillar underneath the play. After the curtain finally fell, Big Bethelites liked to think of the Furlows slipping into eternity holding high the banner of their beloved *Heaven Bound*.

FALL OF A CHOIR, END OF AN ERA

In December 1989 the pastor, McKinley Young, asked the members of the Cathedral Choir to come to an evening meeting at the church. Young had bought them all fast-food chicken dinners—not a specialty of Auburn Avenue cuisine but acceptable just the same. The news that awaited the singers, however, was not so palatable: Young, accompanied by his minister of music, announced that the Cathedral Choir would be disbanded at the end of the month.

The Cathedral Choir had been the last stop for *Heaven Bound* old-timers and a repository for former members of Choir Number One and Choir Number Two. All the fun, struggles, and triumphs of the past must have flashed before these old-timers when Young made his announcement. There was heated discussion, with pleas and tears, but Young was not moved. Citing lack of cooperation as the reason, he brought an end to ninety-two years of choral tradition in Big Bethel Church. And the claim that the singers had staked on the play was finally broken.

"ALL THERE TOGETHER"

The sanctuary was prettiest on a weekday afternoon, when the sunlight brought out the full glory of the stained-glass windows. The church seemed filled with memories, especially in the fall of the year, when momentum gathered for yet another performance of the play. "If walls could talk," I thought, as my imagination flashed back through the rich history of the church, filling its empty aisles with the bygone heroes and heroines of the play. Daisy Brown, the Hypocrite, first described the eerie feeling that filled the church as *Heaven Bound* time approached: "We're all there together." It was a feeling of deep communion encircling all the players—old and new, living and dead. The last scene of the play, its beauty and pageantry vivid in the mind's eye, evoked that feeling of communion. "Now, all the ransomed hosts of God are gathered with the angels," the Scroll Reader would say. Then, the Saints, the Pilgrims, and even Satan with all his gang, would come to the front of the church for the

“All there together”—the finale.

grand finale. The perils of Life's Highway behind them, the characters gathered around the great white altar for one last song of triumph. And somewhere from eternity could be heard another choir singing along with these *Heaven Bound* Pilgrims. It was, no doubt, the great choir of the Church Triumphant, filled with yesteryear's Big Bethelites and echoing back the faith and hope of the long journey home: "The best is yet to come! The best is yet to come!"

Afterword

A Just a short walk down Auburn Avenue, Big Bethel was not very far from the house of Sallie Daniel Braswell, my Grandmother Sallie. A devout Big Bethelite and a loyal fan of the play, she always walked to the church to see *Heaven Bound* both nights it was performed. With my hand in hers, she took me for the stroll down Auburn to see the play one autumn night in the early 1950s. The night-time glitter and neon lights of Sweet Auburn made quite an impression on a small boy like me. The Masonic lodges, the WERD radio station, and Hawks Dinette—all alive with people—were visible along the way. After passing the Auburn Avenue Rib Shack and then Yeomans Billiards, I knew my favorite stop was next—Yates and Milton's drugstore, where Grandmother might buy me an ice cream cone. Upon arriving at the church, I could see the parking lot at Hall's Service Station, already filled with the cars of playgoers. Grandmother thought *Heaven Bound* would be good moral training for my soul, and the years ahead would prove her right.

Although I often saw Henry Furlow around Big Bethel Church, I, like most people, came to know him best as Satan in the play. In his presence, however, I dared not call him anything but Mr. Furlow. When I became a teenager, I was assigned to Furlow's world history class at David T. Howard High School, which was named for a former slave who had been a mentor of Big Bethel. One day in class Furlow asked me to try out for a role in the play as one of the Gamblers. I agreed.

My decision to become involved with the play was wise, if not providential. *Heaven Bound* was more than a message about good and evil, or a story about black music, black literacy, or folk theater. One of the treasures the play offered was the opportunity to work alongside some wonderful human beings. The deepening rapport with responsive audiences and the strong bonds between the players affected me deeply. Like so many others who grew up in the play and found their lives redirected by it, my own life was never the same again.

I well remember the first time I tried out for the part of one of the Gamblers. I was fifteen years old, nervous, and completely inexperienced as an actor. All the old-timers were whispering instructions to me at once. Florine Furlow, who was seated at the piano, smiled graciously as I finished my clumsy efforts and gladly went back to my seat in the pews.

After about three years in the play, I became a student at nearby Emory University. The "rational" environment of the university led me to a naive cynicism and made me question the existence of Heaven. I could not make the "by-and-by" fit my own vain logic. Indeed, to my mind, the play had become mere entertainment, and the whole business of religion, questionable. I tried to understand intellectually what my elders had come to know fully in their hearts. I was puzzled by their shouting, their moaning, their heads nodding yes to something I could not feel.

But one autumn night in the mid 1960s I was struck with the spiritual might of the play. While peeping out from Hell after playing my part I saw Evvie Mabry playing the role of the Determined Soul. Henry Furlow had said, "Nobody does it like Ester Jordan," but I questioned his assessment as I listened to Mabry sing "I'm Going Through." My goose pimples gave way to an uneasy, uncanny excitement. For the first time I began to understand the ultimate purpose of the play.

Evvie Mabry brought home to me the higher power of the play. A highly intelligent woman, Mabry had worked most of her life as a practical nurse. In her nineties she enchanted her guests by reciting, in a low, rich voice, passages from Edgar Allan Poe's "The Raven" or "Annabel Lee." Mabry, whose years in Big Bethel Church spanned nearly the entire twentieth century, could remember the days when Mother Butler used to explode with the spirit in the Sunday morning worship services. "I want some of what Mother Butler has," Mabry recalled saying to herself. A gifted pianist and composer, Mabry often told how she came to write music: "The spirit would descend on me in the middle of the night and write whole songs—note by note—in my mind." There were always a few people like Evvie Mabry in the church and throughout the black experience—people guided not so much by the light of reason as by the power of divine revelation. Into the play, and into the role of the Determined Soul, she brought this divine power.

Like so many others for whom the play was a turning point, I seemed to find my spiritual crossroads in Mabry's performance. A profound sense of change came over me as I watched her. It was a powerful feeling that could not be analyzed or even expressed in words. I only felt a power radiating throughout my entire being, and I knew that it was real. "I set my eyes on Heaven," said Mabry just before stepping into the spotlight, "and I don't let anything turn me around." I was truly spellbound watching Mabry step down Life's Highway. Her white robe was resplendent in the spotlight, her praying hands clasped firmly together in front of her. Proud and erect, she went forth singing the song of the Determined Soul, leaving me and others with these words lingering on our lips and in our hearts:

> Lord, I have started to walk in the light,
> Shining upon me from heaven so bright,
> I've bade the world and its follies adieu.
> I've started in Jesus, and I'm going through.

As the producer and sometimes director of *Heaven Bound,* I have had the task of trying to manage the play toward the twenty-first century. Unlike the work of my predecessors, which involved maintaining the secrecy surrounding the play and raising money to relieve church debt, my work has kept me face to face with the challenge of keeping the play alive. The changes in the community, the shifting congregation, and the rapid succession of pivotal events at Big Bethel have made the job a daunting and formidable task. In 1992 McKinley Young, the steward of fundamental change at the church, left for South Africa, where he would assume his first assignment as a newly elected bishop. The Cathedral Choir, which Young had disbanded, had transformed itself into a social club, content to wait in exile, as it were, for the arrival of a new pastor. While the ousted old singers hoped for some form of reinstatement, new church members continued to join the younger choirs, the Voices and the McKinley Young Choir. From the ranks of these choirs, new members gradually made their way into the play.

Clearly, the approaching end of the twentieth century has been a time of transition for the church. The uncertain direction of all the changes has raised tough questions that overcast the future of the play. Can the upcoming *Heaven Bound* generation come to terms with the glory of the play's past—the spirituals, the old faith, the great crowds? And the old-timers—can they lift their hopes to the play's future, a future that promised few returns to the past? With all the changes, will it even be possible to preserve the essential flavor of the play?

Several ideas have been pursued in search of answers. A good bit of the play's rehearsal time was devoted to talk sessions in which the cast explored the purpose, meaning, and tradition of each role. Experts in music and drama were summoned from Atlanta University to train and critique the Celestial Choir and the Pilgrims. In several outstanding performances, the college founded at the church, Morris Brown, sent its own choir to join Big Bethel's.

Although these expedients have shored the play up and kept it going, the next chapter in the story of the play cannot yet be written. That chapter will have to await another author at another time. Meanwhile, I take my place with the rest of the cast, looking to the future with high expectations. Like those first players of 1930, who started out six Satans, four directors, and almost eight hundred performances ago, I fully entrust the future of the play to Him whose work it is.

Appendix: Players and Participants

Although I have attempted to make this compilation of participants as complete as possible, it remains incomplete: members of the Celestial Choir were seldom listed in the programs (their names became known only after they came out of the choir to take other roles), and programs for some years cannot be located. Thus there are gaps.

Ebony Abercrombie: orphan, 1991
Fatima Akbar: orphan, 1988–90
Crystal Ammons: angel, 1990
Karen Ammons: Mother's Girl, 1993
Laura Ammons: Wayward Girl, 1990
Dorothy Anderson: Mother's Girl, 1970

Chris Bagley: orphan, 1993
F. D. Bailey: angel, 1938–44
Martha Bailey: angel, 1937–62; saint, 1973
Marribell Baker: saint, 1960–75
M. Banks: Determined Soul, 1938–44
Lois Bearden: Mother in Heaven, 1955, 1962
Odessa Cummings Beasley: Pilgrim of Sorrow, 1970, 1974–78, 1983, 1985–86, 1989
Surnelia Bell: angel, 1955, 1960, 1962
P. Harris Benjamin: gambler, 1988–90, 1993
John Bigsby: Pilgrim to Heaven, 1930; Wayworn Traveller, 1930–37
Josephine Bigsby: Mother in Heaven, 1930, 1938–49
Charles Bishop: Pilgrim of Faith, 1949–60
Willie Bolden: gambler, 1938–44
George Bolton: gambler, 1947–62
James Booker: orphan, 1967
Montressa Boulware: angel, 1990
Waymon Bray: Soldier in the Army of the Lord, 1933–82; chorister, 1970–82
Mary Stewart Brinkley: saint, 1967–74
Clarence Brown: Rich Man, 1967, 1970
Daisy Payne Brown: Hypocrite, 1942–83
Evangeline Brown: orphan, 1967
Fred Brown: Preacher, 1987
James Brown: scroll reader, 1937
Marie Brown: angel, 1960–67
Robert Brown: gambler, 1973–75, 1978, 1983, 1985
Olean Bussey: Mother in Heaven, 1967, 1970, 1974, 1975, 1976; angel, 1974–76
Rosalyn Bussey: Mother's Girl, 1974, 1975, 1976?; angel, 1983

Sarah Caldwell: scroll reader, 1974–83
Nietta Campbell: Widow, 1949, 1955
William Carter Carey: Pilgrim of Faith, 1945–48?
Horace Carney III: orphan, 1975–76, 1978
Meishawn Carney: orphan, 1975–76; angel, 1978
Weymonn Edge Carney: orphan, 1947, 1949; Christian, 1973–83; organist/pianist, 1988
Sadie Cash: Widow, 1987–91
Audrey Chambliss: Christian, 1983, 1985
Addie Champion: Bedridden Soul, 1937

Susie Chapman: Burden Bearer, 1947; Pilgrim of the Cross, 1955–85
Thelma Charleston: angel, 1985–93
Courtney Clark: orphan, 1985; Mother's Girl, 1990
Denise Clark: angel, 1985
Eric Clark: Saint Peter, 1993
W. C. Clark: Pilgrim of Faith, 1930–42?
Mamie Cleveland: angel, 1930–50
Viola Cleveland: Mother in Heaven, 1938–44
Lena Cobb: angel, 1967–78
Deilia Cockburn: angel, 1989–93
Patricia Cockburn: Christian, 1986, 1988, 1992; Pilgrim of Sorrow, 1988–93
Gerald Coleman: gambler, 1987–90
Gregory D. Coleman: gambler, 1963–93; producer, 1986–93
Jeffrey Coleman: gambler, 1989–90, 1993
Kevin Coleman: gambler, 1988–90
Meredith Coleman: orphan, 1991, 1993
Nannie Coleman: angel, 1967; Pilgrim to Zion, 1985–93
Shelia Coleman: angel, 1991
Edna Collier: Widow, 1970, 1974–76, 1978; saint, 1985–86
Calvin Collins: orphan, 1937 and before
Maureen Cooper: angel, 1955; Widow, 1960, 1962
Sujette Fountain Crank: scroll reader, 1985–93
Luel Cummings: Saint Cecelia, 1967; angel, 1970–78
Odessa Cummings. *See* Odessa Cummings Beasley

Carolyn Daniels: Saint Cecelia, 1978, 1983
Mary Dansby: saint, 1960–75
Josephine Davis: organist/pianist, 1956–85
Nellie Lindley Davis: Soldier in the Army of the Lord, 1930; Wayward Girl, 1930–43; director and chorister, 1930–43
Raymond Dean: gambler, 1937
Theresa Deavers: angel, 1938–42
Gabrella Wise Dewberry: angel 1930–83
Lena Dean Douglas: Bedridden Soul, 1988–93
Carol Dove: orphan, 1955
Pearlie Dove: angel, 1955
Harry Dukes: gambler, 1967
Raleigh Durden: Reformed Drunkard, 1983?, 1985–93
Georgetta Dye: angel, 1986–93
Reginald Dye: orphan, 1985–90

Gwen Edge: angel, 1986, 1989
Waymon Edge: Rich Man, 1947, 1949, 1955, 1960, 1962
Weymonn Edge. *See* Weymonn Edge Carney
Clara Edwards: organist, 1930–45
Leila Edwards: angel, 1955–67
Harriett Elder: scroll reader, 1955–68
Lizzie Elliot: saint, 1960
Harriette Enous: organist/pianist, 1947–90
Emellen Estes: scroll reader, 1960–73
Devries Evans: Pilgrim to the Promised Land, 1960
Ruby Evans: Determined Soul, 1967
Ruby Morris Evans: Pilgrim to the Promised Land, 1968?

Cynthia Fikes: Burden Bearer, 1991
Susie Fikes: Pilgrim of the Cross, 1989–93
E. Fisher: angel, 1968
Dorothy Buggs Flemister: Pilgrim to Zion, 1937–44; Determined Soul, 1947–62
William Flemister: orphan, 1955
Hallie Franklin: Pilgrim of Sorrow, 1930–36
Deborah Freeman: scroll reader, 1985–86
Florine Dyer Furlow: organist/pianist, 1930–87
Henry J. Furlow: Satan, 1933–84; chorister, 1944–84; director, 1947–85

Martha Garner: angel, 1955–85
Victor Gay: chorister, 1988–92
Morris Gillon: Reformed Drunkard, 1960–78, 1983?
Robert Glass: Saint Peter, 1937
Frances Glenn: Bedridden Soul, 1967–83
Anita Brown Glover: Mother's Girl, 1955–78
Frank Glover: Saint Peter, 1985–86
Carmel Green: angel, 1956
Herman Green Jr.: orphan, 1967, 1970, 1975–76
Jacquelyn Green: Saint Cecelia, 1970–76; angel, 1978, 1983; Hypocrite, 1986–87, 1989–93
Julius Green: lighting and sound, 1950s-90s
Mabel Green: angel, 1967
William Green: lighting and sound, 1950s
Bernice Gross: Pilgrim of the Cross, 1938–44; Wayward Girl, 1945–60

Glenn Halsey: chorister, 1987, 1989
Melanie Hannans: Mother's Girl, 1991
Deangelo Hardy: orphan, 1991
Arthur Harris: Reformed Drunkard, 1937–42
Gloria Harris: angel, 1976
Bettye Harrison: angel, 1978
Charlie Hawkins: lighting and sound, 1940s–70s
Louis Hawkins: Rich Man, 1937 and before; Saint Peter, 1938–75
Mattie Hawkins: angel, 1937–49
Evalyn Henderson: orphan, 1978, 1983
Harold Henderson: Satan, 1976–86, 1993
Willa Henderson: scroll reader, 1983
H. J. C. Hightower: Satan, 1972–74
A. D. Hodges: Pilgrim to Heaven, 1930; Reformed Drunkard, before 1938
Doris Moreland Holiday: angel, 1960, 1962; Wayward Girl, 1963–87
Samuel Holiday: Saint Peter, 1973–83
Florine Hooks: angel, 1985–88, 1990
Belle Hubbard: Pilgrim to Heaven, 1930; Pilgrim of the Cross, 1930–37; Bedridden Soul, 1938
Lavern Hudson: angel, 1938–67
Lucy Hudson: Hypocrite, 1937–42
Deborah Hutchinson: angel, 1983–91

Elizabeth Ingram: angel, 1955, 1960
Chuck Irving: orphan, 1988–90
Leroy Irving: Rich Man, 1973–87, 1991, 1993
Pearlene Irving: Widow, 1993

Victoria Jackson: angel, 1983; Widow, 1985–86; Mother in Heaven, 1987
Pearlene James: angel, 1985, 1986
Arsula Jenkins: saint, 1975–78
Ernestine Johnson: Determined Soul, 1974–93
Ralph Johnson: Striver, 1962–87, 1990
Calvin Jones: Striver, 1989
Clarissa Jones: angel, 1978–86
Coy Jones: Preacher, 1938–44; Striver, 1947, 1949, 1955, 1960
Huellen Morgan Jones: angel, 1947; Pilgrim of the Cross, 1953; Pilgrim to Zion, 1955–68
Janie Dawson Jones: Mother's Girl, 1938–49, 1960
Lottie Jones: saint, 1960, 1962
Louise Jones: saint, 1967–78
Louise J. Jones: Burden Bearer, 1975–90, 92–93
Lula Byrd Jones: Pilgrim to Heaven (later Pilgrim to Zion), 1930
Monica Jones: Hypocrite, 1991–93
Nellie Jones: angel, 1983–93
Olivia Jones: Wayward Girl, 1944
Ruby Jones: Determined Soul, 1970
Rubye Morris Jones: Pilgrim to the Promised Land, 1930–37, 1985

Tammy Jones: Mother in Heaven, 1978
Vernon Jones: chorister, 1985–93; Reformed Drunkard, 1985–93
Esther Jordan: Pilgrim to Heaven, 1930; Determined Soul, 1930–38

Eugenia Keaton: Christian, 1932–37
Dorothy Kelsey: angel, 1978–93
Lanell Kennedy: angel, 1991
Carlos King: orphan, 1987
Ernest King: Pilgrim of Faith, 1986–91
Jessie King: gambler, 1970, 1976, 1978
William King: gambler, 1976, 1978

Gwendolyn Langley: Mother's Girl, 1985
Jacquelyn Langley: Mother in Heaven, 1985, 1988, 1990–91
Mr. Lark: Rich Man, 1938–42
Harriet Lemons: Widow, 1938–42
Mary Lemons: orphan, 1937 and before
Pet Lewis: angel, 1937
Willie Lewis: Pilgrim to Zion, 1949
Olivia Little: Pilgrim of Sorrow, 1930–36
Christine Lloyd: Pilgrim to Heaven, 1930; Pilgrim of Sorrow, 1931–36
Ruby Lloyd: angel, 1930–60; scroll reader, 1938–49; Saint Cecelia, 1960, 1962
Hannah Lovelace: Hypocrite, 1930–36
Daisy Lowe: Pilgrim to the Promised Land, 1987–93
Kelly Lowe: orphan, 1988–90; gambler, 1991

Evvie Smith Mabry: Determined Soul, 1962, 1974
J. D. McBride: Striver, 1938–42
Willie Mae McConnell: saint, 1985, 1986; angel, 1990
Lois McCray: angel, 1983
Monte McCullough: orphan, 1983
Esther McDonald: saint, 1975–86
Nanette McGhee: Saint Cecelia, 1983–88
Ann McKenzie: Pilgrim of the Cross, 1980–93
Haroldeen Murray McMullen: Pilgrim to Zion, 1967–1976, 1978; organist/pianist, 1967–83; chorister, 1973–83; Soldier in the Army of the Lord, 1983
Candace McNeir: Pilgrim to Zion, 1988
Kevin McNeir: Preacher, 1986
Carlton Maddox: orphan, 1988–90; Pilgrim to Zion, 1990–93
James Maddox: Satan, 1986–93; Striver, 1988
Michael Mann: orphan, 1960, 1962
Pamela Mann: orphan, 1960, 1962
Phillip Mann: orphan, 1960, 1962
Robert Mason: Wayworn Traveller, 1985–93; Preacher, 1987, 1988–93
Lonnie Massengill: Saint Peter, 1988, 1990
Helen Massey: angel, 1947, 1949
Henry Matthews: Saint Peter, 1930–34
Don Meteye: orphan, 1955
Charity Collins Miles: Widow, 1947
Essie Miller: angel, 1988–90
Lona Watson Minor: angel, 1930–62
Patricia Moore: Saint Cecelia, 1993
Dorothy Moreland: angel, 1960
Lillian Moreland: Burden Bearer, 1949–74
Dora Morgan: Pilgrim to Zion, 1947, 1953
Huellen Morgan. *See* Huellen Morgan Jones
Louise Morris: angel, 1991
Ruby Morris: orphan, 1937 and before
Rubye Morris. *See* Rubye Morris Jones
Harold B. Murray: gambler, 1953
Haroldeen Murray. *See* Haroldeen Murray McMullen
Lena Murray: angel, 1955, 1960, 1962
Odeen Murray: angel, 1949–78

Lucille Neely: angel, 1970, 1973–76, 1978, 1983–86
Harolyn Nelson: Christian, 1987, 1991, 1993

Leslie Nolan: Pilgrim of Sorrow, 1938–44, 1960, 1962; chorister, 1948–70

Alecia Oden: angel, 1983, 1991
Willa Cleveland Owens: Burden Bearer, 1937–44

Lena Parker: Pilgrim of Sorrow, 1937
Johnette Elder Parks: angel, 1955; Wayward Girl, 1962
Lacy Patrick: angel, 1991
Josephine Peak: Widow, 1937 and before
Gwendolyn Pearson: angel, 1955
Albert Pettis: Striver, 1937
William Petty: scroll reader, 1985–93
Phillips children: orphans, 1938–42
Louise Phillips: angel, 1955–85
Renita Phillips: Christian, c.1938–70
W. Phillips: orphan, 1947, 1949
Camelia Pierson: angel, 1988–89
Willie Pope: orphan, 1960
Effie O'Neal Porter: Pilgrim to the Promised Land, 1955–78
Mary Price: Hypocrite, 1985–88
Georgia Pritchett: Determined Soul, 1985–90
Walter Pritchett: Saint Peter, 1983, 1989–91
Wyolene Pullum: director, 1945–47
George Pullum: Satan, 1930–32; Wayworn Traveller, 1934–62

M. Reese: angel, 1947, 1949
Geneva Ricks: Bedridden Soul, 1960, 1962; saint, 1986
Millard Roberts: lighting and sound, 1930s, 1940s
Bessie Robinson: angel, 1991
Marie Robinson: angel, 1967
Mary Robinson: Mother in Heaven, 1993
Mona D. Robinson: angel, 1985–88; Pilgrim of Sorrow, 1986; Saint Cecelia, 1989–91
Ruby Robinson: Mother's Girl, 1930
Willie Louise Robinson: angel, 1983, 1988
Leroy Russell: Preacher, 1947–76

Glenn Samuels: Striver, 1991–93
Albertine Sauls: scroll reader, 1970
Willie Scofield: Wayworn Traveller, 1967–93
Christine Scott: angel, 1960, 1967, 1970
Emma Scott: organist/pianist, 1987–93
Jamal Ship: orphan, 1993
Robert Shorter: gambler, before 1968
Phillip Skerrett: organist/pianist, 1990–93
Mildred Smith: Pilgrim to the Promised Land, 1983; Soldier in the Army of the Lord, 1985–91
Rosa Stafford: Pilgrim of Sorrow, 1967; Saint Cecelia, 1968
Deborah Stephens: Mother's Girl, 1993
L. Stephens: angel, 1968
E. Stokely: Pilgrim to the Promised Land, 1947, 1949

Samuel Tanks: Rich Man, 1974; Wayworn Traveller, 1975–83
Faustina Tate: Mother's Girl, 1974
Jason Thomas: orphan, 1988–90; gambler, 1991
Mary Thomas: Christian, 1985
Nina Thompson: Pilgrim of Sorrow, 1987; Pilgrim of Faith, 1991–93
Mattie Thrasher: Bedridden Soul, 1985–88
Sallie Tinsley: Pilgrim of the Cross, 1947, 1949
Gloria Tinubu: director, 1988, 1990
Barbara Troup: angel, 1955, 1960

Candace Ushery: Pilgrim of Sorrow, 1988–93

Jo Ann Bearden Vickers: angel, 1960–82; Hypocrite, 1983; director, 1985–87, 1989, 1993

Marie Wainwright: angel, 1955

Norris Walters: Preacher, 1983, 1985–86; Soldier in the Army of the Lord, 1988–93
Opal Walters: angel, 1988–93
Cathy Ward: orphan, 1970
Edward Warmsley: Preacher, 1937 and before
Kwajelyn Washington: Wayward Girl, 1991–93
Eva Watson: Widow, 1983
Lona Watson. *See* Lona Watson Minor
Vicki Watts: angel, 1991
Addie Weavers: Pilgrim to the Promised Land, 1938–44
Gloria West: angel, 1978
Wendall Whalum: chorister, 1983–85
Carlysle White: orphan, 1978
Carmel White: angel, 1960
Mamie White: angel, 1938–44
Vera White: angel, 1985, 1986
Ophelia Whitehead: angel, 1955
Lanie Williams: angel, 1938–42
Sarah Williams: Pilgrim to Heaven, 1930; Soldier in the Army of the Lord, 1930–31
Freddie Wilson: saint, 1962
Ophelia Wilson: angel, 1960–87
Al Wise: orphan, 1975–76; gambler, 1985, 1986
Gabrella Wise. *See* Gabrella Wise Dewberry
Gabriella Wise: orphan, 1947, 1949
Gloria Wise: angel, 1955
Cora Wofford: angel, 1970–76; Bedridden Soul, 1989
Virginia Wood: Wayward Girl, 1988–90
Ebenezer Woods: Pilgrim of Faith, 1961–85
Avril Woodson: Mother's Girl, 1983?, 1985
Shirley Woodson: angel, 1974–85
Estella Wright: scroll reader, 1930–36
Joseph Wyatt: orphan, 1970

Dallesteen Yates: Mother's Girl, 1986–87
Carrie Young: Pilgrim to Zion, 1983
Dorothy Young: Mother in Heaven, 1983, 1985–86, 1988–90
Joyce Young: Pilgrim to the Promised Land, 1985–88, 1993; Mother's Girl, 1988–89
Karen Young: Mother's Girl, 1983?
Roland Young: Satan, 1985, 1986
Stephanie Young: orphan, 1991
Thandiwe Young: orphan, 1983, 1985; angel, 1990

M. Zachary: angel, 1947, 1949
Charles Zanders: gambler, 1938–75; Preacher, 1978
Charlie Zanders Jr.: orphan, 1947, 1949
Ernestine Zanders: angel, 1947–67

Notes

The following notes to the text are keyed by page and line number.

3.1–2: Zelda F. Popkin, "*Heaven Bound* Authentic Negro Folk Drama Out of Old Savannah," *Theatre Guild,* 6 August 1931, 15; 3–4: "Heaven Bound," *Time,* 10 August 1931, 40; 6: William E. Schmidt, "Flocking to Pageant's 'Pearly Gates,'" *New York Times,* 10 November 1985.

21.34–35: Richard R. Wright, *Bishops of the A.M.E. Church* (Nashville: AMEC Sunday School Union, 1963), 94.

22.4–5: Wright, 56; 9–11: Eileen Southern, *The Music of Black Americans,* 2d ed. (New York: Norton, 1983), 77; 23–31: Wright, *Bishops,* 17–18.

25.1–8: *Jones v. Howard,* testimony of Lula B. Jones, 1, 4–8; defendant's exhibit D, early handwritten notes of Nellie Davis entitled "Foreword"; 9–10: depositions of Lula B. Jones and Henry M. Jones, 20 April 1931, 12.

29.21–26: *Jones v. Howard,* affidavit of Mary Brinkley, 21 April 1931; 27–33: deposition of H. M. McBride, 10 April 1931, 3; 37: testimony of Lula B. Jones, 1.

30.1–3: *Jones v. Howard,* testimony of Lula B. Jones, 1.37.16: "Heaven Bound," *Time,* 10 August 1931, 40.

37.17–18: "*Heaven Bound* to be Given Soon to Help Miles," *Atlanta Daily World,* 25 December 1931, 7.

38.3–5: Margaret Hamilton Richards, "Big Bethel Gives Opera," *Atlanta Journal,* 9 November 1930; 8–11, 39.1, 6–7: *Jones v. Howard,* H. Jones affidavit, 30 April 1931,

39.4–6: Richards, "Big Bethel Gives Opera"; 6–7: *Jones v. Howard,* H. Jones affidavit, 30 April 1931; 39–40: Martha Scott Garner, interview by author, Atlanta, Ga., 1 September 1989.

40.22–23: Clifford M. Kuhn, Harlon E. Joye, and E. Bernard West, *Living Atlanta: An Oral History of the City* (Atlanta: Atlanta Historical Society; Athens: University of Georgia Press, 1990), 95.

42.16–17: Kuhn, Joye, and West, 111.

47.1–4: *Jones v. Howard,* depositions of Lula B. Jones and Henry M. Jones, 20 April 1931, 20; deposition of Nellie Davis, 20 April 1931; 11–12: plaintiff's exhibit B.

48.6–7: Popkin, "*Heaven Bound,*" 14.

50.29–36: *Jones v. Howard,* affidavit of Lula Jones, 27 April 1931.

51.10–17: *Jones v. Howard,* affidavit of Henry Jones, 30 April 1931.

53.21–27: *Jones v. Howard,* affidavit of Ruby P. Lloyd, 24 April 1931; 34–38: affidavit of Ruby D. Morrison, April 1931.

54.17–31: *Jones v. Howard,* affidavit of Lula Jones, 27 April 1931; testimony of Lula B. Jones, 11; affidavit of Lula Jones, 27 April 1931; testimony of Lula B. Jones, 7; affidavit of Lula Jones, 27 April 1931; testimony of Lula B. Jones, 8.

55.3–5: *Jones v. Howard,* deposition of Nellie Davis, 20 April 1931, 15; 10–15: affidavit of Nellie Davis, 14 May 1931; deposition of Nellie Davis, 20 April 1931, 12, 3, 6; 17–27: deposition of Nellie Davis, 20 April 1931, 8, 9.

55.5–6: "Heaven Bound," *Time,* 10 August 1931, 40.

57.10–11: John Hope Franklin and Alfred A. Moss Jr., *From Slavery to Freedom,* 6th ed. (New York: Knopf, 1988), 341.

62.38–41, 63.1: Edna Akers Collier, interview by author, Atlanta, Ga., 21 August 1989.

67.26–37, 69.1–4: Medora Field Perkerson, *"Heaven Bound," Atlanta Journal Magazine,* 29 August 1937, 9.

69.5–7: Frank Daniel, "Detailed Staging of *Heaven Bound* Planned Here," *Atlanta Journal,* 8 August 1937; 7–8: Gamewell Valentine, "Scenery Impressive in *Heaven Bound* World Music Critic Finds after Seeing Religious Pageant at Atlanta Theatre," *Atlanta Daily World,* 12 August 1937; 9–10: Perkerson, *"Heaven Bound,"* 9; 11–13: Mozelle Horton Young, "*Heaven Bound* in Brand New Garb Hailed by Capacity Audience," *Atlanta Constitution,* 11 August 1937; 20–24: Perkerson, *"Heaven Bound,"* 9; 25–30: Young, "*Heaven Bound* in Brand New Garb"; 37–39: "Negro Play Stops Drawing When WPA Pretties It," *Chattanooga News,* 12 February 1938.

75.11–23: "Many Pay Last Respects to Mrs. Nellie L. Davis," *Atlanta Daily World,* 6 June 1944.

85.2–4: Henry Furlow, interview by WAGA-TV, a local television news station, videotape, Atlanta, Ga., 2 November 1978.

92.1–5: James Cone, *God of the Oppressed* (New York: Harper and Row, 1975), 115.

102.18–24: Popkin, *"Heaven Bound,"* 17.

104.4–5: E. Franklin Frazier, in *The Negro Church in America,* by E. Franklin Frazier; *The Black Church since Frazier,* by C. Eric Lincoln (New York: Schocken, 1974) 57; 6: Langston Hughes and Arna Bontemps, eds., *The Book of Negro Folklore* (New York: Dodd, Mead, 1958), 289.

107.1–3: *The Plymouth Traveler* (1965), quoted in "Big Bethel African Methodist Episcopal Church: A Century of Progress and Christian Service," 1968.

112.3–4, 117.13–15: Evvie Smith Mabry, interview with author, Atlanta, Ga., 4 April 1990.

132.37–41: Popkin, *"Heaven Bound,"* 16.

134.34–36: Bill Baker to H. J. Furlow, 15 August 1937, H. J. Furlow–Florine Dyer Furlow Collection, Atlanta–Fulton County Library Special Collections, Atlanta, Ga.

135.6–10: Quoted in Sibley, "Time Again for *Heaven Bound," Atlanta Constitution,* 4 November 1987; 28–34: *The Bicentennial Book of Discipline of the African Methodist Episcopal Church* (Nashville: AMEC Sunday School Union, 1984), 17.

136.21–24: Bill Buchanan, "'Pearly Gates' Swing Open for Church Musical Here," *Atlanta Journal and Constitution,* 7 November 1971.

145.1–2: Mabry, interview.

152.4–6: Florine Furlow, conversation with the author, Atlanta, Ga., 1983.

156.25–27: Schmidt, "Flocking to Pageant's 'Pearly Gates.' "

160.36–41: Esther McDonald, interview by author, Atlanta, Ga., 31 May 1989.

163.4–6: Sibley, "Time Again"; 16–24: Sibley, "Big Bethel Church's *Heaven Bound* Is Joyfully Unchanged," *Atlanta Constitution,* 31 October 1988; 35–37: Henry Furlow, videotaped interview.

Bibliography

BOOKS

Atlanta City Directory. vols. 22, 31, 37, 61. Atlanta: Atlanta City Directory Co., 1922, 1931, 1937, 1961, respectively.

Baldwin, Lewis V. *There Is a Balm in Gilead: The Cultural Roots of Martin Luther King, Jr.* Minneapolis: Fortress Press, 1991. For a brief discussion of the churches in Atlanta's Auburn Avenue community and the probable influence of Big Bethel's *Heaven Bound* on King.

The Bicentennial Book of Discipline of the African Methodist Episcopal Church. Nashville: A.M.E. Sunday School Union, 1984. A general statement by Richard Allen and a bicentennial statement of recommitment to a religious order that reflects the black experience in America.

Boylston, Elise Reid. *Atlanta, Its Lore, Legends and Laughter.* Doraville, Ga.: Foote and Davies, 1968. For brief comments about the Atlanta Union Sabbath School.

Carter, Edward R. *The Black Side: A Partial History of the Business, Religious and Educational Side of the Negro in Atlanta, Georgia.* Freeport, N.Y.: Books for Libraries, 1971. General historical comments about black Atlanta through 1894 and the history of the Big Bethel congregation.

Cone, James. *God of the Oppressed.* New York: Harper and Row, 1975. For a discussion of the theology of oppression and of the search for God through the experience of black song, sermon, and folklore.

Franklin, John Hope, and Alfred A. Moss Jr. *From Slavery to Freedom.* 6th ed. New York: Knopf, 1988. A comprehensive history of blacks in America, including particular mention of the factors that gave rise to the Harlem Renaissance.

Frazier, E. Franklin. *The Negro Church in America;* C. Eric Lincoln. *The Black Church since Frazier.* New York: Schocken Books, 1974. A sociological analysis of the African American church in America.

Frazier, Thomas R., ed. *Afro-American History: Primary Sources.* New York: Harcourt, Brace and World, 1970. For a short collection of spirituals and brief comments on the religion of the slaves as expressed in the spirituals.

Garrett, Franklin M. *Atlanta and Environs: A Chronicle of Its People and Events.* Vol. 1. 1954. Reprint. Athens: University of Georgia Press, 1969.

Hepburn, Lawrence R. *The Georgia History Book.* Athens: Institute of Government, University of Georgia, 1982. For discussion of race relations and economic conditions in Georgia in the early twentieth century.

Hughes, Langston, and Arna Bontemps, eds. *The Book of Negro Folklore.* New York: Dodd, Mead, 1958. For a collection of the spirituals, gospel songs, and black folk tales.

Kuhn, Clifford M., Harlon E. Joye, and E. Bernard West. *Living Atlanta: An Oral History of the City.* Atlanta: Atlanta Historical Society; Athens: University of Georgia Press, 1990. For a discussion of African Americans in Atlanta in the 1930s and 1940s.

Lincoln, C. Eric. *The Negro Pilgrimage in America.* New York: Bantam Books, 1967. A short history of blacks in America.

McGill, Ralph. *The South and the Southerner.* 1963. Reprint. Athens: University of Georgia Press, 1993. For a description of the southern white point of view relative to race relations.

Mapson, J. Wendell. *The Ministry of Music in the Black Church.* Valley Forge, Pa.: Judson Press, 1984. For a biblical, theological, and historical perspective on the role of music in the black worship experience.

Miller, Arthur R., and Michael Davis. *Intellectual Property, Patents, Trademarks and Copyrights.* St. Paul: West Publishing Co., 1983. For a summary of copyright law.

Schoener, Allen, ed. *Harlem on My Mind.* New York: Random House, 1968. Pictures and newspaper clippings depicting Harlem before, during, and after the Harlem Renaissance.

Shavin, Norman. *Atlanta: Triumph of a People.* Atlanta: Capricorn, 1982. For an abstract of Big Bethel's ancestral churches and the origin of Morris Brown College. (The dates cited for the fire in the church are unreliable.)

Singleton, George A. *The Romance of African Methodism.* Nashville: A.M.E. Press, 1985. A comprehensive history of the A.M.E. Church.

Southern, Eileen. *The Music of Black Americans.* 2d ed. New York: Norton, 1983. A comprehensive history of African American music, including discussions of Richard Allen's influence on the music of the early black church and of the origin, nature, and importance of the spirituals and gospel.

Thurman, Howard. *Deep River and the Negro Spiritual Speaks of Life and Death.* Richmond, Ind.: United Friends Press, 1975. An account of the religion and theology captured in the spirituals.

Woll, Allen. *Black Musical Theatre, from "Coontown" to "Dreamgirls."* New York: Da Capo Press, 1989. A survey of theatrical works of the Harlem Renaissance.

Wright, Richard R. *Bishops of the A.M.E. Church.* Nashville: A.M.E. Sunday School Union, 1963. For discussions of the Heaven-focused early black church and the pioneering vision of the bishops of the early A.M.E. Church.

ARTICLES

Journals

Fletcher, Winona L. "Witnessing a 'Miracle': Sixty Years of *Heaven Bound* at Big Bethel in Atlanta." *Black American Literature Forum* 25 (Spring 1991): 83–92. For a review of the qualities of *Heaven Bound* that explain its sixty-year survival; an examination of the racial makeup and reaction of its audience; and a comparison of the play with *The Green Pastures.*

Keenan, Hugh T. "*Heaven Bound* at the Crossroads: A Sketch of a Religious Pageant." *Journal of American Culture* 11 (Fall 1988): 39–45. A historical sketch of the play, with mention of the effect white directors had on it.
Suggs, Redding S., Jr. "Heaven Bound." *Southern Folklore Quarterly* 27 (December 1963): 249–66. For a comparison of *Heaven Bound* with medieval morality plays.

Newspapers and Magazines

"Angel Falls Out of Heaven." *Atlanta Constitution,* 11 August 1937.
"Atlanta Theatre News—*Heaven Bound* to Finish Week." *Atlanta Constitution,* 13 August 1937.
"Bethel's Sacred Play to Be Given Tonight." *Atlanta Constitution,* 27 February 1931.
"Big Bethel Benefit Program Announced." *Atlanta Constitution,* 28 March 1923.
"Big Bethel Choir 26 Years Old Today." *Atlanta Journal,* 23 February 1947.
"Big Bethel Choir Hits New Heights At Pops Concert." *Atlanta Constitution,* 28 July 1947.
"Big Bethel Choirs Heaven Bound Again." *Two Bells,* 23 October 1972.
"Big Bethel Church Swept by Fire, To Be Rebuilt at Once." *Atlanta Journal,* 17 February 1923.
"Big Bethel Fire Destroys Church." *Atlanta Constitution,* 17 February 1923.
Buchanan, Bill. " 'Pearly Gates' Swing Open for Church Musical Here." *Atlanta Journal and Constitution,* 7 November 1971.
Collier, Bert. "How A Baby Upheld Law for Big Bethel." *Atlanta Journal Magazine,* 11 March 1923.
Daniel, Frank. "Detailed Staging of *Heaven Bound* Planned Here." *Atlanta Journal,* 8 August 1937.
Davis, Frank Marshall, ed. *Atlanta Daily World,* 4 December 1931, p. 4.
"Diabolical Doings in Atlanta." *Life,* 26 January 1953.
"*Green Pastures* Now in Frisco." *Atlanta Daily World,* 28 May 1932.
"Harry Pace Attaches Salary of *Green Pastures* Actor." *Atlanta Daily World,* 11 December 1931.
"Heaven Bound." Time, 10 August 1931.
"Heaven Bound." Life, 17 May 1943.
"*Heaven Bound* Director Coming Here." *Atlanta Daily World,* 1 January 1932.
"*Heaven Bound* Opens Thursday at Big Bethel." *Atlanta Daily World,* 3 November 1985.
"*Heaven Bound* Return Worth Shouting About." *Intown Extra,* 24 October 1985.
"*Heaven Bound* to Be Given Soon to Help Miles." *Atlanta Daily World,* 25 December 1931.
"*Heaven Bound* to Be Staged at Auditorium." *Atlanta Daily World,* 23 May 1932.
"Many Pay Last Respects to Mrs. Nellie L. Davis." *Atlanta Daily World,* 6 June 1944.
"Negro Play Stops Drawing When WPA Pretties It." *Chattanooga News,* 12 February 1938.
"On the Road to Glory Land." *Atlanta Journal and Constitution,* 9 November 1990.
"Pageant to Have 610th Performance." *Atlanta Journal,* 9 September 1945.
Perkerson, Medora Field. *"Heaven Bound." Atlanta Journal Magazine,* 29 August 1937.
Popkin, Zelda F. "*Heaven Bound* Authentic Negro Folk Drama Out of Old Savannah." *Theatre Guild,* 6 August 1931.
"Presenting Three Hundred Thousand Dollars Worth of Property." *A.M.E. Christian Recorder,* 25 October 1945.

Reynolds, I. P. "What Sam of Auburn Avenue Says." *Atlanta Daily World,* 5 May 1932.

Richards, Margaret Hamilton. "Big Bethel Gives Opera." *Atlanta Journal,* 9 November 1930.

Schmidt, William E. "Flocking to Pageant's 'Pearly Gates,'" *New York Times,* 10 November 1985.

Sibley, Celestine. "Tricky, Sporty Old Scratch." *Atlanta Constitution,* 3 November 1953.

———. "*Heaven Bound* Sinning Appears Pretty Clear Cut." *Atlanta Constitution,* 9 November 1959.

———. "Does The Devil Make Him Do It?" *Atlanta Constitution,* 17 October 1978.

———. "Time Again for *Heaven Bound.*" *Atlanta Constitution,* 4 November 1987.

———. "Big Bethel Church's *Heaven Bound* Is Joyfully Unchanged." *Atlanta Constitution,* 31 October 1988.

———. "Morality Play Has Place in History." *Atlanta Journal and Constitution,* 5 November 1989.

———. "*Heaven Bound* at 60 More Special Than Ever." *Atlanta Constitution,* 5 November 1990.

———. "This Is What 'Heaven' on Earth Sounds Like." *Atlanta Journal-Constitution,* 3 November 1991.

———. "An Angel Gets Her Wings and a New View of Heaven." *Atlanta Constitution,* 13 November 1991.

"Spelman Schedules Langston Hughes for Lecture." *Atlanta Daily World,* 11 December 1931.

Valentine, Gamewell. "Scenery Impressive in *Heaven Bound* World Music Critic Finds after Seeing Religious Pageant at Atlanta Theatre." *Atlanta Daily World,* 12 August 1937.

Young, Mozelle Horton. "*Heaven Bound* in Brand New Garb Hailed by Capacity Audience," *Atlanta Constitution,* 11 August 1937.

BIG BETHEL A.M.E. CHURCH PUBLICATIONS

"Big Bethel African Methodist Episcopal Church: A Century of Progress and Christian Service." 1968. Booklet.

"Big Bethel African Methodist Episcopal Church Anniversary Celebration, Theme: Our One Hundred and Thirty-fourth Year: Another Milestone in Our Pilgrimage of Faith and Service." 1981. Booklet.

"Big Bethel African Methodist Episcopal Church, 'Celebrating Our Christian Commitment to the Church and the Family.'" 1986. Brochure.

"Big Bethel A.M.E. Church, One Hundred and Fifteenth Anniversary." 1980. Brochure.

"Big Bethel African Methodist Episcopal Church, One Hundred Forty-first Anniversary, Family Worship, 'Salvation for Today—Spiritual Hope for the Future.'" 1988. Brochure.

"Big Bethel A.M.E. Church, One Hundred and Thirteenth Anniversary." 1978. Brochure.

"Big Bethel African Methodist Episcopal Church, One Hundred Thirty-sixth Anniversary Celebration, 1847–1983." 1983. Brochure.
"Big Bethel African Methodist Episcopal Church, Second Annual Lay Fellowship Dinner." 1982. Brochure.
"Big Bethel African Methodist Episcopal Church, Third Annual Lay Fellowship Dinner." 1983. Brochure.
"Big Bethel Florine Dyer Furlow, Harriette Baynes Enous Organ Concert Series 1988." April 1988. Brochure.
"Big Bethel Weekly Bulletin." 1930. Circular.
"Men's Day Observance, Big Bethel A.M.E. Church, Theme: 'Men Dedicated to Christ.' " 1979. Brochure.
"Richard Allen, Founder of the African Methodist Episcopal Church." 1981. Brochure.
"The 109th Atlanta-North Georgia Annual Conference, The African Methodist Episcopal Church, Sixth Episcopal District." 1983. Brochure.

OTHER PUBLICATIONS

"Combined Minutes of the 43rd Quadrennial Session of the General Conference of the A.M.E. Church." Fort Worth, Texas, July 6–14, 1988.
Fulton County Superior Court. Real Estate Information. Records Room\Deeds. Deed for the sale of land on which stood Bethel Tabernacle owned by Lemuel P. Grant, February 24, 1869. Deed book L, page 339. Atlanta, Ga. 1990.
Lula B. Jones v David T. Howard, et al. Equity no. 623, RG 21, GI 17004, U.S. Dist. Ct. N.D. Ga., May 1932, box no. 515-517, B49/12/23. National Archives, SE Region, East Point, Ga.
Rubin, Michele McNichols. "The Great American Pie: Theatre as a Social Force in Race Relations in Contemporary America." Ph.D. diss., Emory University, 1984.

COLLECTIONS

Atlanta–Fulton County Library Special Collections, Atlanta, Ga. H. J. Furlow–Florine Dyer Furlow Collection. For *Heaven Bound* pictures, newspaper clippings, and letters from fans.
Big Bethel A.M.E. Church, Atlanta, Ga. Financial Ledgers. 1924, 1933. The Minutes of the *Heaven Bound* Committee Meetings. 1971–1984.

INTERVIEWS AND PERSONAL COMMUNICATIONS

Bearden, Lois. Interview by author. Atlanta, Ga., 31 May 1991. Recollections of Auburn Avenue during the 1950s and a discussion of Harold Bearden's opinion of the play.
Brown, Thelba. Telephone conversation with author, 9 July 1991. Recollections of his boyhood and a description of the mood of the congregation during World War II.

Burris, Evelyn. Interview by author. Atlanta, Ga., 3 September 1989. Information about Bernice Gross.

Butler, N. Marguerite. Telephone conversation with author, 2 October 1990. Biographical information about Florine Furlow.

Cobb, Lena, and Cora Wofford. Interview by author. Atlanta, Ga., 3 July 1989. Recollections of the early enthusiasm of the cast and a discussion of parishioners who worked for wealthy white Atlantans.

Collier, Edna Akers. Interview by author. Atlanta, Ga., 21 August 1989. Details of the 1937 performance at the Atlanta Theatre in 1937 and Choir Number Two's performance at the premier of *Gone with the Wind* in 1939; telephone conversation with author, 6 October 1990.

Cooper, Imogene. Telephone conversation with author, 1 March 1991. Recollections about Mamie Cleveland.

Enous, Harriette. Telephone conversation with author, 15 October 1991. Information about *Heaven Bound*'s organists.

Furlow, Henry, and Florine Furlow. Interview by Hugh Keenan. Atlanta, Ga., 4 April 1982. Comments about the origin and purpose of the play and the Furlows' roles in it.

Furlow, Henry, and L. J. Jones. Interview by author. Atlanta, Ga., November 1978. Reflections on Furlow's role as Satan and Furlow's anticipation of an afterlife in Heaven.

Furlow, Henry, and L. J. Jones. Interview for WAGA-TV. Videotape. Atlanta, Ga., 2 November 1978.

Garner, Martha Scott. Interview by author. Atlanta, Ga., 1 September 1989. Recollections of performances of *Heaven Bound* by Atlanta churches other than Big Bethel.

George, Carrie. Interview by author. Atlanta, Ga., 10 January 1992. Comments about Nellie Davis and information about the unpublished writings of others in Atlanta's black churches during the Harlem Renaissance.

Green, Julius. Telephone conversation with author, 5 October 1990. Recollections of his reaction after reading a *Life* magazine article about the play while he was in the navy during World War II.

Henderson, Harold. Telephone conversation with author, 9 July 1991. Recollections about his role as Satan.

Hightower, James. Telephone conversation with author, 9 July 1991. Recollections about his role as Satan.

Holiday, Sam. Telephone conversation with author, 9 March 1991. Biographical information about Doris Holiday.

Johnson, Ralph, and Corinne Johnson. Interview by author. Atlanta, Ga., 25 May 1989. Their memories of more than fifty years at Big Bethel.

Jones, Henry, Jr. Interview by author. Atlanta, Ga., 29 June 1989. Recollections of Lula B. Jones at the time she filed her lawsuit against Big Bethel, and for his description of her reaction when she was expelled from the choir; interview by author. Atlanta, Ga., 17 September 1989.

King, Mary Ruth Talmadge. Interviews by author. Atlanta, Ga., 15, 20, and 22 October 1991. For a review, with the author, of pictures and brochures and for descriptions of the events leading to the construction of the present sanctuary.

Mabry, Evvie Smith. Interview by author. Atlanta, Ga., 4 April 1990. General recollections about *Heaven Bound* and Big Bethel in the early 1900s.

McDonald, Esther. Interview by author. Atlanta, Ga., 31 May 1989. Recollections of church life around the time of the 1923 fire and for recollections of the first performance and of significant events throughout the history of the play.

Moreland, Lillian. Telephone conversation with author, 9 March 1991. Biographical information about Doris Holiday.

Nix, Fannie. Interview by author. 3 September 1989. Recollections about the earlier years of the Daughters of Bethel.

Payne, Daisy Brown. Interview by author. Atlanta, Ga., 29 June 1989. Details about Nellie Davis's personality, social life, illness, and death.

Illustration Credits

The author and publisher are grateful to the following individuals and institutions for permitting the reproduction of the photographs included in this book.

Pages ii, H. J. Furlow and Florine Dyer Furlow Collection, Atlanta Public Libraries, by permission of Pearlie Dove for the Estate of Florine Dyer Furlow; 26, Big Bethel A.M.E. Church; 30, Thelma Jones Belt and Henry Jones Jr.; 31, National Archives, SE Region, East Point, Ga.; 38, Reprinted with permission from the *Atlanta Journal* and the *Atlanta Constitution*; 41, Hollins Photography, Atlanta, Ga., Big Bethel A.M.E. Church; 43, H. J. Furlow and Florine Dyer Furlow Collection, Atlanta Public Libraries, by permission of Pearlie Dove for the Estate of Florine Dyer Furlow; 45, photography by Alan S. Weiner, courtesy of Gregory D. Coleman; 58, H. J. Furlow and Florine Dyer Furlow Collection, Atlanta Public Libraries, by permission of Pearlie Dove for the Estate of Florine Dyer Furlow; 60–61, Kelly Photography, Atlanta, Ga., Big Bethel A.M.E. Church; 65, 66, Big Bethel A.M.E. Church; 68, Big Bethel A.M.E. Church; 70, 79, 80, H. J. Furlow and Florine Dyer Furlow Collection, Atlanta Public Libraries, by permission of Pearlie Dove for the Estate of Florine Dyer Furlow; 81, photograph by John Zimmerman, H. J. Furlow and Florine Dyer Furlow Collection, Atlanta Public Libraries, by permission of Pearlie Dove for the Estate of Florine Dyer Furlow; 83, 84, H. J. Furlow and Florine Dyer Furlow Collection, Atlanta Public Libraries, by permission of Pearlie Dove for the Estate of Florine Dyer Furlow; 88 (top), Big Bethel A.M.E. Church; 88 (bottom), H. J. Furlow and Florine Dyer Furlow Collection, Atlanta Public Libraries, by permission of Pearlie Dove for the Estate of Florine Dyer Furlow; 90, photograph by John Zimmerman, H. J. Furlow and Florine Dyer Furlow Collection, Atlanta Public Libraries, by permission of Pearlie Dove for the Estate of Florine Dyer Furlow; 91, H. J. Furlow and Florine Dyer Furlow Collection, Atlanta Public Libraries, by permission of Pearlie Dove for the Estate of Florine Dyer Furlow; 92, courtesy of Herman Mason; 93, H. J. Furlow and Florine Dyer Furlow Collection, Atlanta Public Libraries, by permission of Pearlie Dove for the Estate of Florine Dyer Furlow; 95, H. J. Furlow and Florine Dyer Furlow Collection, Atlanta Public Libraries, by permission of Pearlie Dove for the Estate of Florine Dyer Furlow; 97, Kelly Photographers, Atlanta, Ga., H. J. Furlow and Florine Dyer Furlow Collection, Atlanta Public Libraries, by permission of Pearlie Dove for the Estate of Florine Dyer Furlow; 99, H. J. Furlow and Florine Dyer Furlow Collection, Atlanta Public Libraries, by permission of Pearlie Dove for the Estate of Florine Dyer Furlow; 100, 101, Hollins Photography, Atlanta, Ga., Big Bethel A.M.E. Church; 103, H. J. Furlow and Florine Dyer

Furlow Collection, Atlanta Public Libraries, by permission of Pearlie Dove for the Estate of Florine Dyer Furlow; 104, Gregory Coleman; 110, Jackson Photography, Atlanta, Ga., Big Bethel A.M.E. Church; 115, 116; Hollins Photography, Atlanta, Ga., Big Bethel A.M.E. Church; 118–19, photograph by John Zimmerman, H. J. Furlow and Florine Dyer Furlow Collection, Atlanta Public Libraries, by permission of Pearlie Dove for the Estate of Florine Dyer Furlow; 120, H. J. Furlow and Florine Dyer Furlow Collection, Atlanta Public Libraries, by permission of Pearlie Dove for the Estate of Florine Dyer Furlow; 121, Hollins Photography, Atlanta, Ga., Big Bethel A.M.E. Church; 122–23, Kelly Photography, Atlanta, Ga., H. J. Furlow and Florine Dyer Furlow Collection, Atlanta Public Libraries, by permission of Pearlie Dove for the Estate of Florine Dyer Furlow; 127, H. J. Furlow and Florine Dyer Furlow Collection, Atlanta Public Libraries, by permission of Pearlie Dove for the Estate of Florine Dyer Furlow; 133, H. J. Furlow and Florine Dyer Furlow Collection, Atlanta Public Libraries, by permission of Pearlie Dove for the Estate of Florine Dyer Furlow; 140, H. J. Furlow and Florine Dyer Furlow Collection, Atlanta Public Libraries, by permission of Pearlie Dove for the Estate of Florine Dyer Furlow; 142, photograph by Paul Jackson, Atlanta, Ga., Big Bethel A.M.E. Church; 144, Hollins Photography, Atlanta, Ga., Big Bethel A.M.E. Church; 161, photographs by Paul Jackson, Atlanta, Ga., Big Bethel A.M.E. Church; 162, photographs by Paul Jackson, Atlanta, Ga., Big Bethel A.M.E. Church; 164–65, Hollins Photography, Atlanta, Ga.

Index

References to illustrations appear in italic.